The University of **Law**

14 Store Street
London
WC1E 7DE

How to be an Ethical Solicitor

Putting the principles into practice

Meera Rugarel

Richard Burnham

Published May 2017

ISBN 978-0-9935836-4-3

Bath Publishing Limited
27 Charmouth Road
Bath
BA1 3LJ
Tel: 01225 577810

email: info@bathpublishing.co.uk

www.bathpublishing.co.uk

Bath Publishing is a company registered in England: 5209173

Registered Office: As above

Printed and bound in Great Britain by

Marston Book Services Ltd, Oxfordshire

Contents

How to take the online course

This book is accompanied by an online course which will help to cement the reader's knowledge of the ethical issues discussed.

Each book has been allocated a personal course code which you will need to access the course. Your personal course code is **887231**. Then follow these steps:

(1) Log in to the Bath Publishing website at **www.bathpublishing. com/ethical-solicitor-course.html**.

(2) Click the **Start** arrow and complete your email address and password details.

(3) Click the purple **Start** button and you will be prompted to enter your personal course code (see above).

(4) Then enter your first and last name and click the purple **Start** button again. You will now see the instructions for taking the course.

(5) Click **Continue** and follow the on-screen instructions to answer the questions. You can always go back to previously answered questions if you need to change any answers.

(6) If you want to save what you've done and complete the course later, click **Save and finish later** and confirm that this is what you want to do.

(7) When you want to resume the course, log in to Bath Publishing with the same address as before and click **Log in and resume**.

(8) When you have answered all the questions, click the **Finish course** button and confirm.

(9) Once you have passed the course, click the **Download certificate** button to save it or print it out.

Introduction from the authors

Mena Ruparel

The aim of this book is to spark debate amongst practitioners about the role of ethics in the legal profession. Whilst writing this book the SRA launched its "A Question of Trust" campaign signalling very clearly that the issue of ethics is in sharp focus at the moment. In parallel to that campaign the SRA announced that the Code of Conduct will become less rules-based and more flexible to allow practitioners to make their own decisions where issues arise. There is no doubt that the question of ethics will become an area of increasing attention in the coming years.

As my idea for the book developed, I started to look at the reported cases of misconduct in the legal press. The more I read I noticed that some of the reported cases were ethical breaches that the solicitor may not have committed if they had thought about the ethical/regulatory issues. It seemed to me that solicitors needed a practical approach to the issue of ethics rather than a classical education in theories of ethics. This book does not purport to provide all the answers but it does provide a simple methodology which should assist if an ethical dilemma presents itself.

I invited Richard (who was my paralegal many years ago) to write this book with me as I valued his perspective as a trainee solicitor; not yet "in the system" but with a keen eye on the ethical dilemmas we face in practice. When I initially interviewed Richard I set him a number of ethical dilemmas and was impressed by his reasoning. I value his contributions to the book especially with respect to his approach to the ethics of social media.

We both owe Conor Dempsey a vote of thanks (and a drink) for contributing his wisdom regarding the issues faced by practitioners in the financial services world - he contributed greatly to the chapter on rules-based ethics.

I also owe thanks to a number of solicitors and others who were able to assist in reading, suggesting and general support as I tried to put together my thoughts on this subject; my long-time friend Sarah Newens, Roopa Ahluwalia of Birketts LLP, Lewis Hulatt, Emily Miller from Marshall Walker, The LinkedIn Tutors and Barbara Spoor from Esterase with her wisdom on the Complaints chapter. I have been truly annoying my colleagues at Chapman Pieri Solicitors with regular ethical dilemma questions (and spot tests) - thanks to them all for their patience. Needless to say, my family have been hugely supportive throughout this process, especially my husband Conor who has read many versions of the book.

Richard Burnham

I have always been fascinated by the philosophical clash between legal and illegal and ethical and unethical; I would go as far to say that it is primarily the reason for my interest in the law. Naturally when Mena asked for my assistance in writing this book I jumped at the chance to explore the relationship between law, ethics and regulation in greater detail, particularly in light of the SRA's increased emphasis on ethics and the upcoming amendments to the Code of Conduct.

To expand briefly on Mena's introduction of the book above, we hope that you will use the book in conjunction with the SRA Code of Conduct as a "guidebook" to reflect upon moments where you may be faced with an ethical conundrum and the answer is not immediately clear. As a trainee solicitor I feel that the rules and regulations that surround the regulation of the legal profession require careful navigation, and it is hoped that this book will be of particular assistance to junior members of the legal profession, be they undergraduate law students, LPC students, paralegals or trainee solicitors. As the SRA's regulation becomes increasingly focused on ethics, appreciating the relationship between the law, ethics and regulation is more crucial than ever, and an understanding of their interaction is key from an early stage in every solicitor's career.

I echo Mena's comments that we owe Conor Dempsey (more than one) drink for his assistance in the writing of this book.

Thanks go to my family, and in particular Margaret Burnham, for always instilling a strong understanding of right and wrong in me; Zoe Barnes for the support during the writing process of this book; and Adele Hayes who, in her own words, "has heard enough about that ethics book". Finally I would like to thank my various supervising solicitors during my legal career (their teachings will no doubt have contributed to this book) namely Victoria Copeman, Kellie Williams-Jauvel, Michael Knights and of course Mena Ruparel who has for the best part of five years been ensuring that I do the right thing in my career, for the right reason.

May 2017

Chapter 1: Introduction

"Compliance which compromises ethical standards is not helpful at all. We need to properly define and protect the brand of solicitor. The maintenance of professional standards and ethical behaviour is essential."

Andrew Caplen, President of The Law Society

The view of The Law Society as espoused by the President and that of the Solicitor's Regulation Authority (SRA) is that there needs to be a greater focus by solicitors on the issues of ethics and ethical behaviour. The President indicates that compliance with rules isn't the same thing as behaving ethically, which is something we will return to time and time again in this book. Compliance with a set of rules in isolation to ethical conduct can compromise ethical standards and produce anti-ethical results.

The SRA revealed in Spring 2016 that it is their intention to drastically cut the current version of the Handbook to just 10-20 pages. They propose that there will be two separate Codes of Conduct; The Code of Conduct for Solicitors and the Code of Conduct for Firms. Enid Rowlands, the Chair of the SRA board, indicates that this is to:

"replace detailed and prescriptive requirements with a framework for competent and ethical practice".

Clearly the only way the new regime will work is for all practitioners to have greater understanding and focus on ethics and self-regulation in the context of fewer rules. If the handbook is brief, there will undoubtedly be an expectation that solicitors will be left to make their own decisions about all issues that arise in practice.

The aim of this book is to take a practical look at the ethical challenges that practitioners face in the 21st Century. We have drawn the material for this book from a variety of sources - however it is not our intention to set out a detailed history of ethics starting with Socrates and ending with the SRA. This book should be used as a guide to ethical behaviour and more importantly to ethical thinking and decision-making.

We have used abbreviations for a number of common phrases:

- **COFA**: Compliance Officer for Finance and Administration
- **COLP**: Compliance Officer for Legal Practice
- **IB**: Indicative Behaviours (SRA Code of Conduct)
- **LeO**: Legal Ombudsman
- **O**: Outcomes (SRA Code of Conduct)

- **Principles**: Mandatory Principles (SRA Code of Conduct)
- **SDT**: Solicitors' Disciplinary Tribunal
- **SRA**: Solicitors' Regulation Authority

1.1 The current system

Chapter 2 sets out the issues professions face when they are subjected to "rules-based regulation". Solicitors have moved away from rules-based regulation to "Outcomes-Focused Regulation" (OFR) which was introduced in 2007. The proposed move to reduce the Code of Conduct and Handbook from its current tome of over 400 pages is in keeping with OFR. We now have a draft version of the "New Code" and where we refer to this it will be in the context of the Code of Conduct for Solicitors, for it will be this personal code that will guide every solicitor regardless of who they work for. At the time of writing this is still in the consultation phase and so is likely to change before it is introduced in Spring/Summer 2018. As the New Code is based on the same OFR principles as the current Code, much of what we say will remain applicable when the rules change.

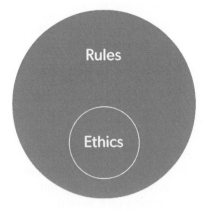

Fig 1: The interaction between rules and ethics under the old Code of Conduct

Lawyers work for the benefit of the public, rather than themselves, their clients, or the courts, and for that reason they must adhere to the ten pervasive ethical Principles:

(1) Justice and the rule of law - a solicitor must uphold the rule of law and the proper administration of justice. Solicitors owe obligations to the court and third parties.

(2) Integrity - solicitors must act with integrity in all professional dealings as they are in a position of trust. They must therefore behave appropriately. This lends itself to the theory of virtue ethics.

(3) Independence - a solicitor must not allow their independence to be compromised. A solicitor should avoid situations which might put their independence at risk.

(4) Best interests of clients - a solicitor must act in the best interests of the client and always act in good faith. In particular the client's affairs should be kept confidential. This relates to the fiduciary obligations a solicitors owes.

(5) Standard of service - a solicitor must provide a proper standard of service to their clients, taking into account the needs of each client.

(6) Public trust - The Law Society and the SRA are keen to improve the reputation of the profession in the eyes of the public. This means that a solicitor must act in a way which maintains the trust the public places in the profession.

(7) Compliance with legal and regulatory obligations - obliges solicitors to deal with the regulators in an open, timely and co-operative manner as well as to comply with their legal and regulatory obligations.

(8) Effective business management - a solicitor must run their business or carry out their role in the business effectively and in accordance with proper governance and sound financial and risk management principles.

(9) Equality of opportunity and respect for diversity - a solicitor must comply with legislation and promote reasonable change.

(10) Protection of client money and assets - a solicitor must protect client money and assets.

1.2   The proposed new system

The New Code of Conduct for Solicitors is not too dissimilar to the current Code. The SRA is staying with OFR, and they believe that having fewer rules will mean more flexibility for individuals but also increased focus on ethical behaviour and outcomes.

Fig 2: The interaction between rules and ethics under Outcomes-Focused Regulation

The initial position paper released by the SRA states that the proposed model for discussion is to set out the core professional principles and a Code of Conduct. Before the announcement about the proposed new Handbook, the SRA opened a consultation called "A Question of Trust" which looked at the ethical behaviour of solicitors and the expectations of the public. The results of the Professional Standards Survey analyses the results of that survey. The survey results make for interesting reading. In conclusion, the authors indicate that:

> *"the SRA have already indicated that they do not see this survey as determining their response to the seriousness of problems; but that it is aimed to help stimulate debate."*

The earliest date the new regulations will come into force is Spring 2018 and firms should be ready for a different approach from the SRA, albeit in keeping with OFR. The content of the guidance in this book won't change drastically as a result of the New Code. Whilst the references to the Handbook will be different, the process of working through an ethical issue will remain the same.

We reference the SRA, the Solicitors Disciplinary Tribunal (SDT) and some light comparison to the regulatory framework of different professions. The status that professionals hold in society means that there are value standards that will be common to them all. The comparison between financial services and legal services is interesting as the professions approach regulation quite differently.

We have taken the decision not to name the individuals whose cases we use as examples from the SDT judgments, which was an ethical decision.

Whilst we can all learn from the mistakes of others, we did not feel that it was necessary at all to put those individuals through any further anguish. Should you wish to read the judgments in full they are on the SDT website (very few judgments are anonymised by the SDT).

Finally we recognise that solicitors practise in different fields, for a myriad of firms and each solicitor has their own way to practise law. Whilst this book deals primarily with solicitors in private practice, it also touches on the challenges of in-house practice. In-house practice brings unique challenges and many more solicitors are now opting to work in-house than ever before. We also draw distinctions between the different challenges of working in a "city" corporate culture and High Street practice. The new Codes will narrow the differences between the obligations on solicitors who work in-house and those in private practice. The introduction of a separate Code of Conduct for Firms ensures that the solicitor's personal obligations are clear cut.

1.3   Using this book

This book can be used as a guidebook for practice or for use where you may require a little help. It can also be used as a way of enhancing your awareness of regulation and ethics in general, and allow you to identify an ethical thought process to respond to a particular situation. We aim to instil ethical thinking in arenas that might challenge you, such as the ethical way in which to use your social media accounts, both personal and business.

What this book does not do is tell you how you *should* react to a situation in order to achieve regulatory and ethical objectives. The answer to an ethical/regulatory situation is rarely ever clear-cut. The best way to react will depend upon a multitude of subjective considerations. There is never one answer to every ethical dilemma. There is usually a range of options that vary from the best to the worst choices.

Subjective variables that may affect a solicitor's decision-making are;

- the size of the firm;
- the individual solicitor;
- the client.

We aim to instil a method of thinking in an ethical manner, which should result in an ethical outcome.

Ethical scenarios

Throughout this book you will find scenario boxes, many of which have been developed from the decisions of the SDT or real life practice scenarios. The purpose of these scenario boxes is to encourage you to think about how you would respond to a situation which may not seem, on the face of it, to be an ethical situation. This is what you can expect to see; many of the examples we use are SDT cases.

Scenario: An outline of a problem faced by a practitioner

SRA rules: Principles/Outcomes/Indicative Behaviours - The Regulatory approach. Chapter 2 on "Rules-based ethics" might be a good place to start for those unfamiliar with the current regulatory framework.

Potential ethical issues/professional breaches: What are the ethical issues that need to be addressed? Being aware of these means that it is more likely that you will take them into account in the decision-making process.

Possible approaches: what are the options? These will be suggested approaches, which could all be within the regulatory framework but have different ethical approaches.

Suggested reaction/steps to avoid: things to look out for or avoid.

Would it make a difference if...?: subtle changes to the initial scenario that aims to test whether your answer would change depending on additional factors.

For example, consider the below entirely fictional and hypothetical example:

Scenario: Fraudulent practice

Facts

Imagine it is 2014. An LLB graduate has a lifelong dream of becoming a solicitor. Unfortunately upon completing their undergraduate degree they are unable to fund the costs of the LPC. Drastically, they hack into the computer of an LPC provider university and enter their name into their database as a student who successfully completed the LPC. A year later they secure a period of recognised training with a High Street firm that solely provides legal aid and qualify upon completion. They practise fraudulently for the next 5 years, demonstrating the same competency as a solicitor and help many vulnerable clients in the process.

Eventually an SRA review of the LPC provider casts suspicion, and eventually the false entry is located. The false solicitor is arrested and spends 2 years in prison for their deception. Upon leaving prison they successfully complete the LPC, having now amassed the funds, and make an application for their character and suitability to be assessed with a view to being legitimised. Imagine you are an SRA admissions officer reviewing this file. Would you approve the application?

SRA Rules: Principles/Outcomes/Indicative Behaviours

Principle 1: A solicitor must uphold the rule of law and the proper administration of justice.

Principle 2: A solicitor must act with integrity.

Principle 4: A solicitor must act in the best interest of each client.

Principle 5: A solicitor must provide a proper standard of service to their clients.

Principle 6: A person must behave in a way that maintains the trust the public places in them and the provision of legal services.

Principle 7: A solicitor must comply with their legal and regulatory obligation.

Outcome (SB1): A solicitor must be of the required standard of character and suitability. At Part 1 of the test, 1.1(a)-(b) concerning criminal offences provides that, unless there are exceptional circumstances, the SRA will refuse an application where a person has been convicted by a court of a criminal offence for which a custodial sentence was received that involved dishonesty and fraud. The suitability test forms part of the SRA Handbook.

Potential ethical issues/professional breaches

Here is an example of where the regulatory and legal situation may conflict with your ethical views. It may be in this scenario that you sympathise with the graduate's situation - maybe you yourself had difficulty funding LPC costs, or you know someone who did. Perhaps you have children experiencing the difficulty of self-funding the LPC. You may be of the opinion that, however wrong the graduate's actions were, they were not acting maliciously by acting as they did.

You may also consider that the graduate demonstrated skills at the same competency as a solicitor and also helped many vulnerable clients who may otherwise not have received the same service. However, the legal and regulatory situation is that the graduate has misled the public, and acted dishonestly and fraudulently for, ultimately, personal gain. In doing so they have also breached many of the mandatory SRA Outcomes.

Possible approaches

In this scenario it is extremely unlikely that there are any "exceptional circumstances" which justify approving the graduate's character and fitness application. The candidate has also demonstrated that they will breach the SRA outcomes. You should reject the application.

Suggested reaction/steps to avoid

Ultimately you should be aware that there will be occasions where ethically you may believe that it is correct to do one thing, where the regulatory and legal position is extremely clear that you should not do this.

Would it make a difference if...?

The graduate did not act of their own violation. A partner in a firm who knew the graduate could not afford the fees suggested that they hack into the LPC provider's database and that, after doing so, they would give them a period of recognised training to allow them to qualify.

1.4 What is ethics about?

When you ask a lawyer about ethics, the response you get will vary from eye rolling, yawning, or rising guilt. Rarely will solicitors passionately debate legal ethical issues.

Whilst ethics is a subject matter that is difficult to define simply, we all make non-legal ethical choices every day. A simple walk through your day will show that many areas of life are governed by ethical thinking and decision-making. From the time that you wake up you start to make choices. Will your morning coffee be made at home using Fairtrade coffee beans or purchased on the way to the office? If the coffee is purchased at a coffee shop do you choose to go to one that pays few taxes in this jurisdiction or the local independent tax-paying coffee shop? Do you wear ethical clothing? Will you choose your lunch based on how far it has travelled to get to your plate? If it is organic food is this really better for the planet and your health and do you care whether the farmer who provided the eggs gets a fair deal from the supermarket selling them to you? Do you travel on foot, cycle, take a bus or drive? Is this choice based on convenience or because you are trying to minimise your carbon footprint? Do you take ethical holidays or live in a carbon neutral home?

Most people are likely to have a view on these everyday choices and the way you make your choices may seem to be an automatic response. If you don't think any of those issues factor into your life it doesn't mean that you are living an "unethical" lifestyle - you are probably an "ethical minimalist". However, the more you think about your everyday choices the more likely you will realise that you have made decisions based on an internal belief system. This may or may not have a religious element, which we do not propose to discuss in this book.

By analogy, the legal/ethical choices you make will also be influenced by your internal belief system. The main difference is that these choices are regularly monitored, controlled and manipulated by third parties in the work environment. This means that sometimes solicitors get caught out doing things that they may not be proud of, hence the references to SDT cases.

"The ethical solicitor" keeps their own ethical/moral belief system in the forefront of their mind and learns to cross check those against the regulatory framework. This means that there is often more than one response to an issue.

1.5   Is it important?

"[The Principles] define the fundamental ethical and professional standards that we expect of all firms and individuals (including owners who may not be lawyers) when providing legal services.

You should always have regard to the Principles and use them as your starting point when faced with an ethical dilemma.[1]"

The requirement for solicitors to behave ethically in modern legal practice is more relevant than ever. We do not intend to go into microscopic detail about the different types of ethical rules that exist but look at the term in a holistic way - this is not a textbook about ethical theories.

Solicitors are still held in fairly high regard, although that has decreased in recent years according to a YouGov poll. Lawyers are less trusted than teachers and doctors but at least we prevail over accountants and bankers.

---

[1] *SRA Handbook (Law Society Publishing, 2015)*

As professionals we hold a position of trust and we must work to hold that position. In this book we draw parallels between different professions as it is of interest to note what they offer the teaching, learning and development of professional ethics, compared with our regulatory bodies.

Ethics training for qualified solicitors is not mandatory which surprises other professionals and the public as there is an expectation that this would be the case. During the undergraduate law course ethics is not taught as a separate subject and so ethics education generally occurs for those who choose to take the Legal Practice Course (LPC). It is worthwhile noting that this may not be the route many solicitors have taken into the profession. If a solicitor qualified before the introduction of the LPC or took a different route into the profession (the CILEx route for example) they may have been exposed to little or no ethics training. That doesn't mean that they behave unethically.

Contrast this with the focus placed on ethics by the Chartered Institute for Securities & Investment (CISI). 20% of their regulatory unit exam is dedicated to the matter of ethics and integrity. In 2013 CISI became the first professional body to require UK candidates to pass an integrity test. They aim to instil the public with confidence that its members act with integrity at all times, "placing integrity before, and above, profitability." Whether there is any link between more robust ethics in its members by passing this exam we can't say, but putting ethics training at the forefront of their training is a statement of commitment to values that the public expect.

Although solicitors may be aware of their general ethical obligations, they may defer to their firm's nominated compliance officer when faced with an ethical/regulatory conundrum. Many solicitors fail to recognise that daily issues have any ethical element to them and that the problem is theirs to solve. This is why ethical thinking is important as it teaches solicitors to identify issues with an ethical element and think through the best response.

It might be obvious to state this but if the courts and justice system lack an ethical foundation then society will lose respect for the system of rules. These rules help to provide a civilised order upon which society is dependent. If solicitors, as officers of the court, are seen to act unethically this will undermine the principle of justice. Members of society will take their lead from legal professionals and see little point in following the rules.

1.6   The relationship between law and ethics

Law is the body of rules determined and enforced by the state. The point of legal rules is to channel undesirable behaviour in society and offer remedies to people negatively affected by the breaches of these rules. The law usually forbids an action, whilst imposing a consequence in the event that that action is taken. Murdering someone is against the law - if a person commits murder then there is a penalty imposed.

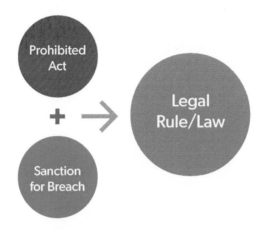

Fig 3: How legal rules are made: prohibit an act and make the breach of it punishable by way of a sanction and you have law

Asking whether something is ethical, and whether that same thing is legal, are two entirely different questions. Ethical principles in law are being increasingly mixed up with regulatory outcomes. The relationship between legal and ethical doctrines is more significant than ever.

This is perhaps a natural progression, as both law and ethics serve to moderate our behaviour; law accomplishes this through the threat of sanction.

Ethics utilise other triggers as a control mechanism; when a person performs an act which is considered to be unethical they tend to feel uneasy. If a vegetarian eats a bacon sandwich they will feel that they have done something wrong, even though it is not illegal to eat meat. Their internal moral code has been broken and they will recognise that even if no one sees them doing it. Leading an ethical, moral life means that one monitors oneself - there is no real threat of sanction to moderate our behaviour.

(1) **Where ethical principles alone are best suited to address behaviour**; morality, but not law, will apply more often in the day to day interaction of society. Being rude and dishonest to others is not illegal, but it may be immoral and unethical. The desire to conform, good manners and good upbringing prevent people from being rude and dishonest.

(2) **Where legal rules are best suited to address behaviour**; there are actions that are illegal, but may not be seen to be unethical. The

issue of assisted suicide may be a good example. Many believe that allowing a person who is terminally ill the right to die is an ethical thing to do. Littering is illegal but may not be seen as unethical.

(3) **Where law and ethics should be deployed jointly**; consider for example theft. This is both illegal under s7 Theft Act 1987, but it is also considered highly unethical to deprive a person of their legally owned property.

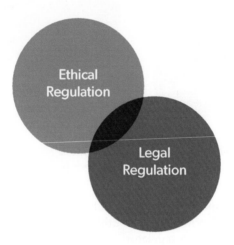

Fig 4: The overlap between ethics and law

Legal rules are considerably more specific than their ethical counterparts - it would be impossible to write down ethical rules as these are contextual and personal. For example, it is unethical to take sweets from a child. However, if the child is diabetic, taking their sweets might be doing them a favour depending on the child's blood sugar levels. It is very difficult to be prescriptive about ethical rules whilst legal rules could not be enforced unless they were written down.

1.7   Different ethics for different people

The question of ethics is a subjective concept. As a result of this the strength of an individual's moral convictions will differ from person to person, and range between a highly ethical person to someone who is unethical or immoral.

An ethical person will consider many ethical principles - in everyday life this person will probably be a vegan who lives in a carbon neutral home.

They will only eat organic vegetables and will probably grow their own food. Their negative impact on the world will be minimal; whilst this might apply to a few people most of us cannot possibly live up to these standards.

In theory, we would hope that no solicitor would be amoral as it would be difficult to practise if one lacked any sense of right or wrong. If a person was naturally amoral they would need to be taught how to operate in a legal system that places great emphasis on ethics.

At the bottom of the ladder is an immoral person, who gives little thought to their ethical responsibility to the rest of the world. Solicitors should never be immoral as this would lead to regulatory challenges very quickly.

Fig 5: How ethical are you?

1.8 How does "the ethical solicitor" practise?

Whilst many solicitors advocate that ethical codes are merely in place to protect clients from the "bad apples" of the profession, most solicitors appreciate that they must discharge their duties as officers of the court in an ethical manner which goes above the ethical response which would be normally expected from a lay member of society. But why is this?

We will explore further, in Chapter 4, that an individual's (i.e. solicitor's) ability to comprehend, or access the tools to comprehend, is crucial to a correctly functioning legal system. Simply put, individuals in society must be able to understand the law in order to avoid breaching it, or, where they are accused of breaching the law, to formulate a defence in order for justice to be seen to be fair. Solicitors therefore hold positions of privilege within society because of the valuable resource they possess; knowledge of the law. This position of privilege can be described as a monopoly which solicitors could, if they so desired, use to extort members of society who are unable to appreciate the complexity of the law without the assistance of legal counsel.

Ultimately the question of "who is an ethical solicitor" engages Principle 2 of the SRA Code of Conduct, and the duty to act with integrity; acting honestly and possessing strong moral principles. This is an extremely onerous demand on a solicitor as what is considered to be dishonest and immoral is subjective and wide reaching.

The concept of the standardised "ethical solicitor" is discussed in significantly more detail in Chapter 3. However, an ethical solicitor will generally:

- know what the right thing to do is;
- act to do the right thing; and
- do so for the right reason.

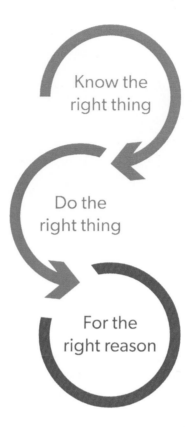

Fig 6: The motto for the ethical solicitor

The ethical solicitor will operate in life, both personally and professionally, with integrity. This is often referred to as "virtue ethics"; how to behave in a virtuous way all the time, not just limited to the practice of law. Virtue ethics is arguably the type of ethics that best applies to solicitors in a system that is increasingly moving away from rules-based ethics.

1.9   Ethics v Compliance

The following questions all operate independently of one another:

    (1)   Is what I'm doing complying with my regulatory obligations?

    (2)   Is what I'm doing illegal?

    (3)   Is what I'm doing unethical?

Fig 7: The interaction between behaving ethically, criminally and in a compliant manner

1.10 Conclusion

All lawyers have a general perception of what "acting ethically" actually is. However, after reading this brief introduction to the concept of ethics and its relationship with the law, you will begin to apply a methodology to approach ethical conundrums. Both concepts can operate as independent regulators of undesirable conduct in society, but it is often the case that both streams will intermingle; legal rules often mingle with ethical concepts and ethical concepts can directly influence the creation of the law.

We conclude that solicitors are subject to higher ethical obligations to society than lay people. Ethics for solicitors can therefore be seen as a hybrid of traditional ethical principles and regulatory requirements, and acting in this way can be said to be acting as an "ethical solicitor". However, as we will explore through this guidebook, how to be an "ethical solicitor" will be subject to various external variables which will fluctuate depending upon the situation at hand. This may make it seem like it is an almost impossible task to be an ethical solicitor. It is hoped that, through the assistance of this book, you will be able to anticipate when you are being faced with an ethical scenario and react appropriately in the circumstances.

Chapter 2: Rules-based ethics

2.1 Introduction

In this chapter, we explore the regulatory matters that every solicitor needs to be aware of. If you happen to be the COLP at your firm then you should already be aware of many of the matters we set out here. For other solicitors not lucky enough to be the COLP this information is very important, by way of background.

We see no need to set out the historic background regarding solicitors' regulation. However, most legal professionals will know that the Legal Services Act 2007 (LSA 2007) has been instrumental in changing regulation for lawyers. This change is ongoing and should be monitored by regulated firms and individual solicitors.

Occasionally in the case studies we refer to the old rules and regulations but we have tried to keep this to an absolute minimum. Solicitors should know that in recent years there have been three sets of rules and codes that might be relevant. There is likely to be another change in 2018 which will see the rules and regulations slashed to a core set of Principles.

Rules	Type of regulation
Solicitors Practice Rules 1990 (SPR 1990)	Rules-based
Solicitors Code of Conduct 2007 (SCC 2007)	Rules-based
SRA Code of Conduct 2011 (SRA Code 2011)	Outcomes-focused
2018: two Codes of Conduct to be introduced	Outcomes-focused

2.2 Ethics and regulation

The interaction between ethics and regulation is a tricky one and best outlined as follows:

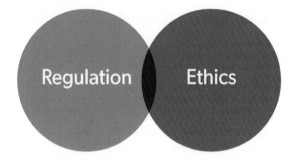

Fig 8: Interaction between rules and ethics

It is easy to envisage a situation in which a solicitor could have a regulatory problem that has no ethical dimension; a straightforward conflict of interest might be an example.

Scenario: Conflict of interest 1

You act for Mrs Patel in employment law matters. Her employer telephones and asks for an appointment. This is a classic conflict of interest issue and is dealt with strictly on a regulatory basis; there is no ethical dilemma at all. The Code of Conduct is clear about this type of conflict; it is not possible for the same firm to deal with employment matters for both the parties.

In a less straightforward conflict matter, the same firm could act for different parties to the same transaction. In these cases the dilemma is to ensure that regulatory issues, such as confidentiality, are properly observed and the "Chinese walls" built to prevent information leaking from one department to another remain robust.

The ethical issues can start when taking on two clients who have similar interests or differing interests in the same transaction. Once that issue is dealt by reference to the regulations, there is then an ongoing ethical obligation to ensure that regulatory issues are properly addressed at all times for each client. In this type of transaction there is likely to be a high level of risk that solicitors need to be aware of. This type of transaction needs to be monitored closely throughout.

2.3   Criminal behaviour, ethics and regulation

The interaction between criminal behaviour, ethics and regulation is complicated but it is important to note that there is an overlap. An example of this would be in the event that a solicitor takes part in a fraud scheme. Although this seems unlikely, there are reported SDT cases of this happening.

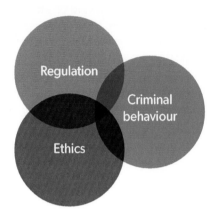

Fig 9: Interaction between regulation, ethics and criminal behaviours

Scenario: Conflict of interest 2

Facts

Solicitor R was involved in an elaborate tax evasion scheme to reduce his client's stamp duty land tax indebtedness to nil on numerous occasions. There were two SDLT "mitigation" schemes that he operated, the success of each which depended on the solicitor failing to disclose information to HMRC about related transactions. In addition, there were Capital Gains Tax "mitigation" schemes that he offered. He wrongly led clients to believe that these schemes had been sanctioned by HMRC when they had not.

Rules

This solicitor had numerous allegations raised against him; he was accused of breaching multiple rules of the Solicitors Code of Conduct, the Solicitors' Accounts Rules, of having conflicts of interest and failing to have a Money Laundering Reporting Officer to name but a few. 161 complaints about the firm had been made to the Legal Complaints Service at the time of the SDT hearing and payments to clients had been made.

Potential ethical issues/professional breaches

The solicitor in question, Mr R, informed the SRA when he was interviewed that he was aware of The Law Society guidelines on property fraud and that he wasn't aware of any instances when he had failed to follow the guidelines. When the SRA wrote to Mr R to ask for details of the schemes he failed to provide this information. The request was repeated, he wrote to the SRA and refused to provide the information to the regulator. He eventually provided some but not all of the information requested.

The Tribunal was satisfied that there had been allegations involving dishonesty against Mr R and this was proved to the higher standard of proof. Mr R was struck off; he offered no mitigation. He was ordered to pay £116,800 in costs to the SRA.

He was pursued by HMRC and criminal matters were brought against him.

Criminal matters

In 2013, he pleaded guilty to seven counts of fraud by false representation and he was sentenced to 2 years imprisonment for each count to run concurrently. These were suspended for two years.

In 2016 Mr R came before the Crown Court under Proceeds of Crime Act offences. He was found guilty and was ordered to pay back £800,000 of the estimated £2m he made from the tax evasion schemes. If he was unable to pay that sum within three months he faced a default jail sentence of up to five and a half months. HMRC said: "*The message is clear: rip off the taxpayer, and we will use the courts to empty your pockets.*"

This is a classic example of a solicitor breaching rules and regulations whilst also being guilty of criminal acts. The regulatory breaches were dealt with first, with criminal matters following over a number of years thereafter.

Ethical issues are central as there is dishonesty at the centre of any fraud - these are not the virtues that the public expects to see associated with a solicitor. This type of behaviour is unethical to say the very least.

2.4   Outcomes-Focused Regulation (OFR)

"The more corrupt the state, the more numerous the laws" (Tacitus)

In October 2011, the SRA moved to an "outcomes-focused" system of regulation that moved away from the old "rules-based" approach. The new approach encompassed a high level outcomes-focused style of regulation (OFR). This also marks a shift away from rules-based ethics towards a more "virtue ethics" style of governance. Your character and reasoning are relied upon to self-govern rather than the expectation that you will follow a strict set of rules.

The focus on outcomes was introduced to encompass a more risk-based approach with the aim of concentrating regulation where it is needed most. The SRA has regularly produced a risk index in order to inform solicitors as to how the SRA views risk and how that can potentially affect firms.

It can be seen that a strict adherence to a rules-based system of regulation can produce perverse "unfair" results for the consumer. The introduction to OFR is intended to ensure that the consumer is protected whether or not there is a specific rule devised for every eventuality or not.

The emphasis is on the quality of outcomes for clients - solicitors must be seen to uphold the law and the proper administration of justice and look to the spirit of the Principles and rules. OFR is intended to be a simpler form of regulation and the SRA strives continuously to reduce the number of rules; it has declared an intention to do this again in 2018. This in turn means that there is a new emphasis on ethics and on maintaining professional standards. Both the SRA and The Law Society have publicly increased their focus on ethics as part of the OFR regime and to maintain the brand of the solicitor. Although it can be difficult to teach professional standards, it is very important that solicitors understand that the introduction of OFR requires a greater application of personal ethics.

2.5   A Question of Trust

In 2015/2016 the SRA launched its campaign, "A Question of Trust" which invited the profession and public to feed back their views of professional standards. SRA CEO, Paul Philip, said: *"This is a landmark campaign that has really engaged people. Regulation is part of the social contract between the profession and the public and it is important that we calibrate and validate what we do."*

The campaign involved live events with the public and a series of online ethics-based scenarios. The SRA indicated that the campaign secured 2,350 online survey responses in addition to which 3,000 people attended their events around England and Wales. The purpose of the campaign was said to be to develop a reference framework for SRA staff when making regulatory decisions. Both solicitors and the public took part in the campaign to assess the seriousness of offences. This is an important piece of work - the results have been published in part by the SRA in the publication of the solicitor's survey result; *Solicitors' Professional Standards* by Cristina Godinho

(UCL) and Richard Moorhead (UCL), which is mentioned elsewhere in this book.

The initial findings from the survey show that criminal activity, dishonesty and misuse of client money rank as the most serious offences with the public. However, solicitors don't rate the issue of their own competence as a serious issue whereas the public do. The public were more likely to rate these issues as being a serious matter whereas solicitors generally saw them as a matter of concern but deserving a lesser punishment.

The results of the survey were said to be inconclusive about the issues that arise in a solicitor's personal life and how or if they should affect their professional life.

Crispin Passmore said of the survey results:

> *"We are considering the findings and are using them to refine our approach to judging the seriousness of offences and what action we might take. We will publish that approach - grounded in the firm evidence of the views of the public and profession - so we can be transparent about our decision-making."*

2.6   Practical operation of OFR

In order to assist solicitors to achieve their regulatory objectives, the SRA has established a framework of 10 Principles, which are mandatory high-level objectives. The Principles are supported by the Code of Conduct, which contains;

- Outcomes; and

- Indicative Behaviours.

These act as guidance to indicate whether solicitors are complying with the regulations. This gives solicitors freedom and flexibility to deliver a range of outcomes in any scenario; the solicitor can then decide which is the most suitable outcome in each case. There are criticisms of this type of regulation from all sides; in-house practitioners do not believe that the current Code deals with their niche practice even with some slight adjustments for them and the same can be heard from magic circle firms and High Street practitioners. The flexible nature of the current regulation doesn't really sit very well with many practitioners who have experienced several years of rules-based regulation. When the rules are black and white it is easy to draw the line and to be able to predict the regulator's actions. When the system relies on your personal interpretation of the best outcome, solicitors feel as though they are being drawn into a trap which is bound to lead them to the door of the SDT.

2.7   Decision-making in the OFR arena

When decisions about right or wrong/ethical or unethical/compliant or not compliant are in the hands of the regulated there is no real certainty of outcome. If your interpretation of the rules doesn't match that of the regulator then there could be serious consequences. Practitioners are uneasy about this type of regulation because it is unpredictable.

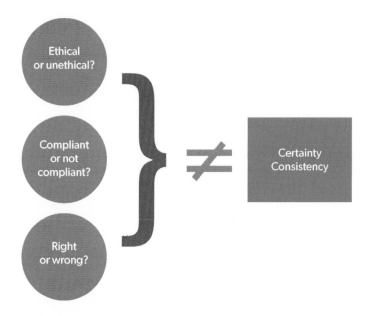

Fig 10: Practitioners need to decide for themselves whether an action is ethical, compliant or right. Each individual decision means that there is no certainty or consistency in outcome

Regulatory decision-making

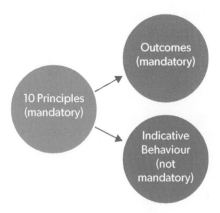

Fig 11: When considering how to make decisions from a purely rules-based approach you would look at the regulatory basics: the 10 Principles always come first, then the mandatory Outcomes and finally Indicative Behaviours

Ethical decision-making

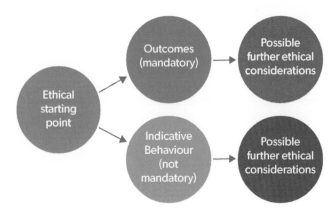

Fig 12: Resolving a problem from an ethical viewpoint is a slightly more complex process. The regulations play a significant role but with additional ethical considerations to be taken into account

2.8   The Principles

(1)   Uphold the rule of law and the proper administration of justice;

(2)   Act with integrity;

(3)   Do not allow your independence to be compromised;

(4)   Act in the best interests of each client;

(5)   Provide a proper standard of service to your clients;

(6)   Behave in a way that maintains the trust the public places in you and in the provision of legal services;

(7)   Comply with your legal and regulatory obligations and deal with your regulators and ombudsmen in an open, timely and co-operative manner;

(8)   Run your business or carry out your role in the business effectively and in accordance with proper governance and sound financial and risk management principles;

(9)   Run your business or carry out your role in the business in a way that encourages equality of opportunity and respect for diversity; and

(10) Protect client money and assets.

When considering ethical issues a solicitor will have their own ethical values - these cannot and should not be erased before approaching a problem, However, in the decision-making process the solicitor should first consider the Principles and the Code of Conduct as these provide a starting point. It is important to note that more than one Principle may be relevant in any dilemma.

In situations where two or more of the Principles conflict the solicitor is expected to come to the conclusion that promotes the public interest and adheres to Principle 1. Ethical considerations, where they are applicable, will be considered with the Principles and Code of Conduct matters.

The Principles apply to everyone working within a regulated entity and this applies to non-solicitor employees. In practice, non-solicitor employees probably know nothing of OFR or their role in the system.

Regulation has moved on to the extent that solicitors can be regulated by the Bar Standards Board, or CILEx regulation instead of the SRA. This is a new innovation and the issues that may be connected to "regulator" shopping are only becoming known now. Individual solicitors are still bound by the SRA's regulatory framework even if the firm is authorised by the BSB. In this book, we are only looking at the SRA regulatory regime which is the most common regulator of choice for solicitors.

2.9   Are ethics and compliance the same?

It is important to remember that compliance and ethics are not the same. This is a central feature of OFR and of this book. Whilst a solicitor may consider the Principles, the Code of Conduct and both the mandatory Outcomes and Indicative Behaviours, the conclusion he or she draws may be compliant but not entirely ethical. This is one of the major reasons that OFR was introduced in the first place.

In an OFR environment, the regulator creates a regulatory framework which sets out the boundaries for solicitors and regulated entities. Since the current regulatory framework is risk-based there are areas which have an increased emphasis on rules. Other areas are more outcomes-focused. In the more prescriptive areas there are direct Outcomes and Indicative Behaviours which means that you either are or are not compliant with the SRA rules. If you are not compliant, you are in breach of the rules and the SRA will address these breaches appropriately. In these circumstances, there is little scope for ethical decision-making. The focus for ethics is in the overlapping areas, where both regulation and ethics have a place. It is then for the individual solicitor to make the ethical case for any particular outcome. Chapter 3 that deals with behaving ethically sets out in more detail how that is approached in practice.

The 10 Principles are the first point of reference for a solicitor considering an ethical dilemma bearing in mind that a particular dilemma can involve more than one of the Principles. When a solicitor considers the Principles, they should ensure that client protection and serving the public interest are both important.

2.10   Considering the Principles and ethical decision-making

The solicitor needs a logical methodology for applying the Principles, considering the priority of conflicting Principles and taking into account the relevant Outcomes and Indicative Behaviours before coming to a decision as to which ethical path to follow. This will make it easier to document the decision-making process and explain the framework for the decision to any interested stakeholders including the client and the SRA.

We have introduced the following motto to guide the solicitor through the decision-making process;

Know the right thing

Do the right thing

For the right reason

The practical approach is as follows;

- Look at the Principles;
- Look at the Outcomes;
- Look at the Indicative Behaviours;
- Apply ethical reasoning to achieve the "right thing".

To demonstrate a logical methodology we will go through the Principles outlining ethical situations that a solicitor may face. We will demonstrate those matters that the solicitor will need to take into account and how the decision-making process should be recorded in the event that the SRA subsequently questions the decision.

Taking each principle in turn, we can see how each affects ethical thinking within the regulatory context.

Principle 1: Uphold the rule of law and the proper administration of justice

Regulated entities should remember that whilst client satisfaction is very important, there is an obligation owed to third parties. Thus when considering ethical conflicts, the solicitor's duty isn't only to their own client. There are wider issues to be investigated as to whether the dilemma involves the rule of law and proper administration of justice.

In the event that Principle 1 is breached it is possible that there will be a criminal breach as well.

Scenario: Criminal breaches

Solicitor J was fined by the SRA when he self-reported a criminal conviction for assault against his wife. Although the incident took place outside of his duties as a solicitor, the SRA's regulatory function includes the regulation of acts undertaken in a solicitor's personal life.

In another example, the SDT dealt with Solicitor K who deliberately gave false evidence at the trial of a High Court action. In doing so, it was her intention to mislead the court, which would be a clear breach of Principle 1. Her transgressions weren't limited to potentially breaching Principle 1 but also Principles 2 and 6.

These examples show that a breach of Principle 1 is serious and may also breach ethical considerations and enter the sphere of criminal wrongdoing. Whilst it is difficult to consider the ethical issues completely separately from the regulatory and criminal issues they are distinct. It is morally/ethically wrong to hit someone and so this is an ethical issue. It is wrong to lie but even more so to lie in court under oath. Many of the criminal matters extend from simple moral and ethical truths.

Principle 2: Act with integrity

A solicitor must act with integrity at all times. There is no definition given to the word, although there are various examples given to this duty by the court and disciplinary body.

The plain language definition of integrity is "the quality of being honest and having strong moral principles". Ethics and morality go hand in hand.

Could it be that the duty is owed to society as a whole, whether or not the solicitor is engaged in professional duties? The answer to this has to be in the affirmative.

The SRA confirm this notion by stating that solicitors are expected to act with integrity in all professional dealings with the client, court and the public. It can be seen from the disciplinary cases and the Code of Conduct as a whole that the duty of a solicitor to act with integrity should be given the widest possible meaning. A solicitor's dealings with the general public in a social situation will require the solicitor to act with integrity which crosses over with the obligations under Principle 6. The solicitor's actions will always be under the scrutiny of the regulator, whether on or off the clock. This extends to interactions with the public via social media, at the pub or exiting a football match.

The ordinary definition leads to another question: is there a difference between ethics and morals?

Are morals and ethics the same thing?

Not necessarily. Morals and ethics are often used interchangeably because the meaning and interpretation of both can sometimes overlap. The standard definition for morals is "standards of behaviour, principles of right and wrong". Added to this that most individuals cannot agree the distinctions between the two words and you end up with two terms of flexible meaning.

Within a professional context, specifically for the legal profession, ethical decision-making needs to be defined. This is to ensure that the profession can be judged to be acting ethically (or not) to maintain public confidence in the justice system. However, in general, ethics are deemed to come from a social system and are dependent on a group definition whilst morals are generally an internal, personal compass of what is right or wrong usually based on a personalised belief system and personal experiences.

This leads to potentially three paradoxical scenarios:

(1) a person following a strict ethical code may not have any morals;

(2) a moral person could violate an ethical code to maintain their morals;

(3) a moral person could select an ethical code to fit in with their moral beliefs.

Therefore a solicitor could easily act according to strong moral principles but not be behaving ethically.

A solicitor who believes that they do not need to buy a train ticket before boarding a train might be committing an ethical breach if they fail to buy a ticket, but they may not be breaching any internal moral code. If their intention is to buy a ticket on the train or before they exit the station then they may believe that there is no lack of integrity on their part and their moral conscience is clear. The regulator is likely to disagree and the train company will have clear rules about when a train ticket must be purchased - these sanctions are inescapable in the event of a breach.

The SRA and potential breaches of integrity

The SRA tends to take a very dim view when solicitors fail to act with integrity. There are many examples of solicitors being sanctioned by the SRA and the SDT for breaches of integrity, for example, failing to buy a train ticket before boarding a train, lying to the police about who was driving a car at the time of an accident, and failing to report a drink driving disqualification to the firm. These are all failures by a solicitor to act honestly in relation to these matters.

Principle 3: Do not allow your independence to be compromised

Some solicitors are of the opinion that their role is to present the client with options in any legal matter. They leave the ethical decision of how to proceed to the client, therefore absolving themselves of having to make the decision. This type of solicitor may be amoral - the choice of the client absolves the solicitor of any ethical culpability. The client will then instruct them what to do without any ethical repercussions for the lawyer as they are following Principle 4 and making the commercial decision to act in the best interests of their client.

However, the solicitor cannot entirely absolve themselves of making an ethical decision or of the possible consequences of their own actions. Other Principles come into play such as:

* Principle 1: uphold the rule of law and the proper administration of justice;

* Principle 3: do not allow your independence to be compromised;

- Principle 6: behave in a way that maintains the trust the public places in you and in the provision of legal services.

Whilst the solicitor acts in the role of adviser to the client the solicitor has the overarching obligation to uphold the rule of law and the proper administration of justice, maintain the public trust in the legal system and not let their independence be compromised. This includes not allowing the clients to make ethical decisions for them so that the solicitor can reap the economic benefits of avoiding making an ethical decision. It is the combination of Principles that provides the framework for decision-making rather than taking individual Principles on their own.

"Lawyers advise - clients apply the ethics" is an easy way for solicitors to practise law but it may be an amoral way to do so. In-house lawyers often struggle with these issues as their client is their employer and their influence can be diluted by financial considerations.

Other solicitors feel that their role is much more directive - whilst they do need to give the client choices, it is for them to strongly steer the client down the "right road" to ensure that the client makes the right decision. This may be by using ADR routes to settle a case rather than to litigate or not using a private investigator in acrimonious divorce proceedings. This might be the approach taken by the "ethical solicitor".

Principle 4: Act in the best interests of each client

It can be difficult to ensure that you are looking out for the interests of each of your clients, particularly if their interests start to conflict with each other.

The issues that solicitors need to be mindful of are where there are 2 or more clients who are each receiving advice from the same solicitor about the same matter or transaction. The solicitor should ensure that each client's interests are considered individually. For example, in a residential conveyancing transaction where the couple are unmarried the solicitor may notice that Party A is contributing the whole deposit which the solicitor believes should be protected. The solicitor needs to carefully balance the advice to both Party A and the co-purchaser Party B who are both clients. The solicitor may morally believe that Party A should ensure that the money is protected in the event of a future relationship breakdown. The way in which this is done is an ethical choice for the solicitor:

Option A: Telephone Party A and make sure they understand that in the event of a purchase as Joint Tenants their deposit may not be protected. Strongly advise them to purchase as Tenants in Common and advise about the preparation of a Deed of Declaration of Trust.

Option B: Speak to both clients together and explain to both of them the advantages and disadvantages of buying the property as either Joint Tenants or Tenants in Common.

Option C: Send the clients an information sheet about purchasing a property jointly and ask them to sign a form notifying you of their decision.

The choice is for the solicitor to make.

Option A is deficient as there is no corresponding advice given to Party B, and this may be a regulatory breach if a complaint is made by Party B who may never be made aware that the conversation took place.

Options B and C ensure that advice is given to both parties - the advice isn't slanted to benefit either party and would meet the regulatory Outcomes. By giving oral advice, the solicitor may be able to stress their own view that this is the best way forward for Party A, and, whilst this might not be welcomed by Party B, they are involved in the conversation. Better still, the solicitor may wish to highlight that this is a potential area for conflict between the clients' interests and that they might wish to seek out separate advice about their relationship and financial repercussions in the event that it comes to an end.

These issues are exacerbated in commercial transactions where one firm is acting for more than one party in a transaction. This is the reason why ethical barriers need to be in place to ensure that client information is protected. If Party A's confidential information is leaked to Party B (also a client of the firm) the firm will be in an ethical dilemma when being required to do the best for each client.

Principle 5: Provide a proper standard of service to your clients

What each solicitor considers to be a proper standard of service can differ between sectors. Ethical issues are manifold when looking at this Principle because the interpretation of "proper standards" will depend on the size of the firm, the type of client and the fees that are being levied.

For example, it was reported in the press that a high profile solicitor charged time for thinking about the client's case in the shower. This is clearly an example of providing a service over and above that which many firms would provide or charge for. This may be a service that high profile multi-millionaire clients expect from their solicitors.

Payne Hicks Beach were quoted in The Telegraph as saying:

> *"In relation to clients, and in particular high profile ones who are often out of the country and lead particularly busy lives, extensive work on complex issues is done at anti-social hours and under considerable pressure."*

Issues arise when the standard of service provided by a solicitor falls short of that expected by the client. Is it reasonable for an "ordinary" client to expect a solicitor to provide a standard of service out of hours and at no or normal cost? These issues are helped by regulatory requirements setting out the handling of a case and the hours that the solicitor will be available. However, in this fast digital age, clients are emailing, Skyping and WhatsApping solicitors at all hours, weekends and bank holidays. The question remains for the solicitor - is this something that they should expect as part of a 21st century "proper standard" of service? The availability of a criminal solicitor out of hours will be expected due to the nature of the job - clients are arrested and interviewed around the clock and so solicitors are expected to be available. A wills and probate solicitor may be required to attend a hospital bedside to take instructions to make an urgent will if someone is on the brink of death. Is an employment solicitor expected to make themselves available at all times just because their colleagues in the criminal department do so? Is it needed and is it a fair expectation to place on them?

Not only does Principle 5 lend itself to a wide interpretation of standards of service, the recent change in the continuing professional development of solicitors places learning and development decisions in their hands. From an ethical standpoint, each solicitor should ask themselves if they are competent within the framework produced by the SRA, known as the Competence Statement. The "ethical solicitor" needs to be able to objectively evaluate their own fitness for the job. This requires strong and virtuous traits, to be able to objectively self-assess one's abilities and pinpoint areas where further development or training is required. Reflecting on one's mistakes and being able to assess them is an important part of the new training regime; these are all ethical judgement calls. This is a huge change from the prescriptive hours based CPD regime that was introduced in the 1980s. Under the current system a solicitor could undertake 6 hours training per year and be perfectly competent to practise. Likewise, another solicitor could undertake 36 hours training per year and still not have achieved competence. This issue is a matter of individual reflection and no longer a tick box exercise.

Principle 6: Behave in a way that maintains the trust the public places in you and in the provision of legal services

Whilst we have mainly been discussing virtue ethics in the context of this book, this Principle leads us to the realms of utilitarianism, meaning how to do the best thing for the majority rather than the individual. Although virtues remain central to this Principle, a solicitor should behave in a trustful way - the stress here is that the public, not just your clients, should trust you.

It is important that all professionals retain a high status in society; professionals hold positions of trust and are held accountable to higher standards than others because of the nature of the work they do. As a result, it would seriously undermine this special status if those virtues were only required to be displayed "on the job". So solicitors must display those virtuous characteristics at all times in order that the public knows that their trust is well placed.

This is a widening of the requirement imposed by Principle 2 and possibly a restatement of it.

Principle 7: Comply with your legal and regulatory obligations and deal with your regulators and ombudsmen in an open, timely and co-operative manner

Although this seems to be a simple direction to ensure that one complies with the regulator, it builds on ethical foundations. In order to maintain the trust the public places on this profession, we must be open to regulation. Without regulation the profession would be viewed as a law with no sanction (often referred to as a "dog with no teeth"). Solicitors must be compliant with requests from the regulator or face sanctions for failure to do so. This is a further focus on virtue ethics - to be open, honest and co-operative with the regulator is more robust than a Principle that requires one to "respond" to the regulator.

Principle 8: Run your business or carry out your role in the business effectively and in accordance with proper governance and sound financial and risk management principles

This Principle focuses much more on sound business foundations than it does on ethics of any nature. It makes sense that the business needs to run effectively and that this should progress on solid foundations. These provisions are especially important for those thinking about starting up a regulated entity.

Principle 9: Run your business or carry out your role in the business in a way that encourages equality of opportunity and respect for diversity

It is a legal requirement that one does not discriminate against other people on the grounds of their race, sex, gender or sexual orientation. This Principle is not a simple restatement of the law on discrimination - it takes matters further than that. The Principle states that a solicitor should act whilst doing his/her job in a way that encourages equality of opportunity and respect for diversity. This is another basis to showcase the strong argument in favour of virtue ethics - solicitors should be positive in the workplace with regard to these matters. The mantra is "encourage equality and diversity" not, "do not discriminate".

There is no test to see how this is implemented in practice. Although the SRA requires firms to publish data on equality and diversity there is no way that they can monitor how this can be encouraged within a firm. It is important that this issue is being addressed by the current Principles even if it can't be tested. Solicitor membership organisations are not under any obligation to publish these types of statistics. It is worth noting that a recent survey suggests that large numbers of barristers' chambers are flouting an obligation to publish their own diversity data. The SRA insists that each firm passes its data to them, whereas the BSB has not imposed a similar burden on its members.

How many firms could say that they actively encourage diversity and equality of opportunity? This is definitely an area of ethical decision-making for firms and an opportunity to stand out from the crowd.

Principle 10: Protect client money and assets

This Principle is the most prescriptive as the Solicitors' Accounts Rules (SAR) set out exactly how client money should be used. Yet, the SDT records are littered with solicitors who have misappropriated client money. In May 2016 the SDT struck off a solicitor for using £45,000 from the sale of a client's property for his own uses. In that case the SDT said, "*the overall catalogue of proven breaches amounted to a masterclass in failure to comply with the basic requirements of practice as a solicitor.*"

We do not propose to look at all of the Outcomes or Indicative Behaviours ("IBs") in the Code of Conduct, save to say that they are an important part of the regulatory system. The Outcomes are mandatory requirements which continue to have an ethical element to them, despite being more rules-based. The IBs are behaviours that tend to show that the Outcomes have been met, whilst not being prescriptive and requiring them to be met on a mandatory basis. For example, a solicitor is required to deal with complaints promptly, fairly, openly and effectively. The IBs indicate that if the firm has a complaints procedure this goes some way to show that the Outcome is being met. We deal with the issue of complaints in more detail in Chapter 6.

2.11 The New Code of Conduct for Solicitors

As mentioned throughout the book, the New Code is not likely to be too different from the old Code as it stays within the OFR model. It is, however, lighter on prescriptive rules and heavier on ethics as is emphasised in the consultation documents. This shows a shift away from the old rules-based ethics and further towards value/behaviour ethics.

All solicitors will have to comply with this Code, irrespective of where they work. In the future, it is likely that solicitors will be employed by firms to deliver non-reserved legal services, which is currently not permitted. The SRA have highlighted that this type of regulation will bring them into line with other legal regulators and with the Institute of Chartered Accountants in England and Wales. The New Code can be referred to as "light touch" regulation as the SRA will only get involved in cases where enforcement action is needed. They emphasise that proportionate enforcement is central to this new era of regulation; a consultation on this issue will inform their approach. They state that:

> *"where we find that solicitors or firms have wilfully, carelessly or negligently misused their freedom, or have abused their position, that response can be robust".*

Solicitors are informed that in the New Code:

> *"You are personally accountable for compliance with the Code - and our other regulatory requirements that apply to you - and must always be prepared to justify your decisions and actions."*

Ethical thinking and decision-making become more important.

The proposed Code for Solicitors is 7 pages long and the Code for Firms comprises only 6 pages.

Principles in the New Code

The SRA propose to retain the Principles in a refined format; the existing 10 Principles may be streamlined to the following 6 Principles:

Solicitors must:

(1) uphold the rule of law and the proper administration of justice;

(2) ensure that their conduct upholds public confidence in the profession and those delivering legal services;

(3) act with independence;

(4) act with honesty and integrity;

(5) act in a way that encourages equality, diversity and inclusion;

(6) act in the best interests of each client.

In the event of any conflict between the Principles, then the Principle that best serves the public interest in the proper administration of justice will take precedence. This remains as it is under the current 10 Principles format.

The following Principles are likely to disappear:

(7) comply with your legal and regulatory obligations and deal with your regulators and ombudsmen in an open, timely and co-operative manner;

(8) run your business or carry out your role in the business effectively and in accordance with proper governance and sound financial and risk management principles;

(10) protect client money and assets.

Not all solicitors work for a firm and so losing these Principles reflects the fact that not all solicitors handle client money or assets or run a business. However, the new Outcomes maintain reference to protecting client money if a solicitor holds it.

The following Principles 5 and 6 appear to be combined and dealt with under the terms of the newly drafted **Principle 2: ensure that your conduct upholds public confidence in the profession and those delivering legal services**:

(5) provide a proper standard of service to your clients;

(6) behave in a way that maintains the trust the public places in you and in the provision of legal services.

The wording of Principle 2 is subject to consultation responses to ensure that it sets the right expectations regarding public trust and confidence.

The provision of a proper standard of service is an issue expanded upon in the Outcomes at section 3 of the Code for Solicitors, which is dedicated to service and competence. Each solicitor is required to ensure that they keep themselves up to date with their professional knowledge and skills.

The remaining Principles have been re-worded; most importantly the new Principle 4 now states that solicitors will act *honestly* and with integrity. The addition of the word "honestly" is an important one to maintain public trust.

The Principle regarding equality of opportunity and diversity changes in the new version:

Current Principle 9: run your business or carry out your role in the business in a way that encourages equality of opportunity and respect for diversity.

New Principle 5: act in a way that encourages equality, diversity and inclusion.

Whereas the old Principle was directed at the running of a business, the new principle focuses on each individual's obligation regarding equality, diversity and inclusion. This is a more onerous obligation on solicitors. Naturally those running a firm regulated by the SRA will be held to the same obligation, so the Principle has been widened. In the Code for Firms this is reflected at O(1.2) which requires firms to publish diversity data as prescribed by the SRA.

The New Code: Outcomes

The SRA will continue to incorporate Outcomes, which are mandatory. However, the SRA will scrap references to Indicative Behaviours in the new Codes.

Some of the IBs will form guidance or part of case studies so that solicitors will have tools to support the slimlined Code of Conduct for Solicitors.

Overlap between the two Codes

The SRA recognises that the following areas overlap duties between the individual solicitor and the SRA regulated firm:

- Referrals, introductions and separate businesses;
- Conflicts of interest;
- Client identification;
- Complaints handling;
- Client information and publicity.

These will appear in both Codes.

COLP and COFA

The roles of the Compliance Officer for Legal Practice (COLP) and Compliance Officer for Financial Administration (COFA) will remain. The scope of these roles will be found in the Code for Firms.

An interesting matter that the SRA mentions in the consultation paper is that the focus on the COLP role *"may (and does) sometimes allow others to abdicate responsibility (thus placing complete reliance on the compliance officer)."* This may be an example of ethical fading; good solicitors sometimes don't realise they're making an ethical choice at all because it is perceived that the COLP is there to make those choices. Making one person responsible for the entire legal practice seems to have the effect of alleviating all others of responsibility and any ethical decision-making functions.

2.12 Comparing ethics in financial services to the legal profession

If you pick up a daily newspaper or surf the news pages on the internet with any regularity you can hardly fail to notice the number of scandals or regulatory investigations the financial services sector has been subject to since the financial crisis in the mid noughties. As a result of this, in order to clean up its act, there has been heavy emphasis on ethical behaviours introduced by the Financial Conduct Authority governing the behaviours of senior management down to the lowliest of employees. Whether this has a lasting effect on the ethical behaviours shown by these institutions or the public perception of them remains to be seen.

Most financial services firms attempt to embed ethics into the culture of their firms. It is not uncommon for prospective employees to sign pledges to behave ethically as part of their employment contracts. Upon the commencement of employment each employee undertakes rigorous compliance training which includes behaving ethically.

The emphasis on ethics and integrity in financial services is understandable. The financial regulators want to protect users of the system and to promote confidence in the same system. Is it so different for the legal world? Solicitors have a massive influence over difficult and stressful situations for individuals and companies. Take for example buying a house, making a will, getting divorced, employment law etc. The general public relies on solicitors to guide them through all of these situations placing these crucial life events in the hands of ethical and honest solicitors.

2.13 Anti-Money Laundering (AML) and Data Protection

There are a number of non-legal areas that are central to the work of all solicitors which require a solicitor to do, or refrain from doing, specific acts. For example, solicitors are required to take great care not to unknowingly or unwittingly assist clients to launder money. The AML regulations are therefore in place to ensure that the solicitor knows what to do when taking on a new client to ensure that money laundering isn't taking place. To know one's client is very important and these regulations cross over to other professions such as financial services.

Similar prescriptive rules are in place to ensure that the client's data is protected and that there are no data breaches, and so the Data Protection Act 1998 sets out a system of rules to govern the proper protection of client data.

These are all specifically rules-based systems with little manoeuvre for interpretation or ethical decision-making. We have therefore decided that these areas won't be covered in great detail here as they are more suitable for a book on regulation.

There are numerous examples in the SDT of solicitors who get caught up in schemes that breach these rules and are punished for doing so. Sometimes the breaches are punished by fines; at other times they are also criminal acts punishable by criminal sanctions.

Scenario: Data protection

Facts

In 2017, Barrister F was the data controller for her business. She was supposed to protect her client's data in accordance with the Data Protection Act 1998 (DPA) and the Bar Standards Code of Conduct which is similar to the SRA Code of Conduct. Both codes require their members to keep their client's information confidential.

Barrister F had created many documents for her clients on her home PC. The report indicates that at least 250 client documents were accidentally uploaded to the internet by her husband who was backing up her computer. He backed up 725 files to an online directory that was not protected and made the documents available via the internet. As soon as this was known to the barrister's husband he removed them from the online directory. The files were visible to the public for a short period but the documents contained sensitive information.

Rules

The reported decision indicates that the data controller was in breach of s4(4) DPA which requires her to keep client data in line with the regulations. She had failed to ensure that she had technical measures in place to prevent third parties accessing the client data - her husband shouldn't have had access to those files at all. She should have encrypted the client files so that even if the data had accidentally been uploaded in the way it was, no one would have been able to view it.

Breaches

In addition to breaching the DPA she was also in breach of her regulator's Code of Conduct, equivalent to Chapter 4 of the Code of Conduct requiring solicitors to keep their client's information secure and confidential.

Outcome

The barrister was fined £1,000 by the Information Commissioner's Office for DPA breaches.

It is not known whether the barrister was also found to be in breach in respect of her duties owed to the Bar Council under the Bar Standards Code of Conduct.

2.14 Summary

Overall, the interaction between the Principles leaves a huge amount of flexibility for the practitioner to operate within. There are some prescriptive, rules-based elements to abide by. Ethics and those qualities associated with virtue and character are central to this type of regulatory system and will hold more importance under the new regime.

Chapter 3: Virtue ethics - behaving ethically

3.1   Do the right thing, for the right reason

Many professionals, not just solicitors, generally aim to behave in such a way that will keep them out of trouble with their regulator. We would suggest that behaving in this way is short-sighted and only requires the individual to meet an end, albeit an important one for professionals. That end goal might be to be "compliant enough" to avoid sanction or just enough to avoid committing a criminal act. To avoid sanction, there is no positive requirement to behave ethically, albeit that this is the general expectation. A solicitor merely needs to avoid the detection of unethical behaviour to avoid sanction - this isn't ethical reasoning.

Behaving ethically means a lot more than just meeting compliance objectives. We will be looking at the positive obligation on professionals to behave in a *positive* ethical way, not only to avoid sanction from the regulator but also to continue to hold the privileged position of being a professional. We suggest that by changing the focus on "positive ethical behaviour", the public will continue to hold solicitors in high regard and perhaps even trust them more.

3.2   Differences in approach

As explained earlier in Chapter 2, prior to October 2011 the Code of Conduct for Solicitors was prescriptive and rules-based. A solicitor merely needed to consult with the Code to understand how they should behave in any given situation. This could lead to situations arising whereby the result is right and governed by the rules but the client is left feeling that the ultimate outcome is wrong.

There is a school of thought suggesting that strict adherence to rules will render unethical situations more likely as it removes the need for solicitors to think about ethics at all.

Post October 2011, the Code of Conduct for solicitors is in line with Outcomes-Focused Regulation (OFR) and this will continue in 2018 when the New Code is introduced. The SRA doesn't want to bind solicitors to a set of strict rules but allow individuals and firms to be able to have the flexibility to make the right choice. Essentially, the solicitor and the firm need to be able to think through a problem and find a solution. This introduces a greater capacity for the individual to think ethically and reach a result which is both compliant and fair to the client.

The way that individuals and firms undertake that process of thinking through a problem is influenced by many factors; the ability to behave ethically in these situations is central to that process under the new regime. Whether this is something that is recognised or not during the thinking process, ethics is central to the way that firms navigate everyday situations.

It is said that solicitors behave in "ethically minimalist" ways and we would hope that solicitors would want to change that perception and behaviour if that is accepted to be the case.

3.3   Ethically minimalist solicitor's motivators

Fig 13: The ethically minimalist solicitor is doing the least that they can to remain compliant and avoid criminal sanctions

We propose that the better way to deal with issues in practice and any ethical dilemma would be the following three point approach:

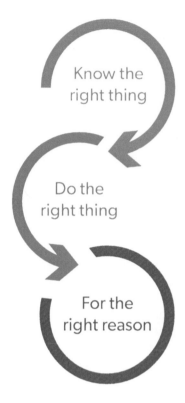

Fig 14: A process motto for the ethical solicitor

Principle 2: Act with integrity

We will not cover the regulatory aspects of Principle 2 in this section - that has already been dealt with in Chapter 2. However, Principle 2 is possibly the main foundation for a solicitor's ethical behaviour. It is wide ranging as it applies to a solicitor's behaviour in all walks of life, not just in practice. Whilst it may be onerous to act with integrity in one's professional *and* personal life, that is what is expected of a professional and especially of a solicitor. It is not unheard of for a solicitor to be struck off the roll of solicitors for acts that took place entirely outside of professional life and unrelated to client matters.

Principle 2 is usually taken together with Principle 6, which places an obligation on a solicitor to behave in a way that maintains the trust the public places in them and in the provision of legal services. These two Principles together ensure that all aspects of a solicitor's behaviour both in work and off the clock are governed by the Code of Conduct.

Acting with integrity more specifically means that solicitors are expected by the public to behave in a way that is;

- Transparent;

- Honest;

- Open; and

- Fair.

In the context of the financial services profession, integrity has been defined as follows;

> *"In our view, "integrity" connotes moral soundness, rectitude and steady adherence to an ethical code. A person lacks integrity if unable to appreciate the distinction between what is honest or dishonest by ordinary standards."*[2]

If we equate the obligation to act with integrity with the parallel and overlapping notion that solicitors should act ethically, we find that such conduct applies to solicitors whether they are in private practice or in-house. This difference should have less distinction when the SRA introduces the New Code of Conduct for Solicitors. Solicitors who work in different geographical areas and different practice areas have different challenges. However, the same Code of Conduct applies to all.

In a recent study[3] solicitors indicated that the top six personal virtues that an ideal lawyer should have were:

(1) Judgement;

(2) Honesty;

(3) Perseverance;

(4) Perspective;

(5) Fairness;

(6) Teamwork.

The top two of these personal virtues help us to understand the central foundation of "the ethical lawyer"; one who is able to respond to dilemmas in an ethically appropriate way, not one who only has an eye on compliance.

3.4 Types of behaviour generally recognised as being unethical

From the list of virtuous characteristics above, we can easily see that there

---

[2] *Hoodless and Blackwell v FSA (Financial Services & Markets Tribunal)*

[3] *Virtuous Character for the Practice of Law - The Jubilee Centre for Character and Virtues (James Arthur, et al)*

are types of behaviour that we should all agree are unethical;

- Lying/dishonest behaviour to court, client or third party;
- Misleading the court, client or third party;
- Failing to protect the client's assets and wider interests.

However, there are times when it is possible that you have done one or all of the above things. It can be difficult for a solicitor to admit to their own unethical behaviour.

To illuminate ethical problems that solicitors face we will use examples from the SDT to outline this behaviour, albeit restricted to the regulatory environment. This means that we are limited to looking only at behaviour that has come to the attention of the regulator and which they decided to pursue. Obviously, this means that there are many other behaviours that either haven't been considered serious enough to pursue by the regulator or that haven't come to the regulator's attention at all. We will attempt to look at all aspects of ethical behaviour and not just that which is serious enough to attract attention. If one acts as an "ethical solicitor" it actually means to act with virtue and integrity in all aspects of one's life and not just the professional context.

In the context of regulatory sanction, the worst ethical transgression to accuse a solicitor of is dishonesty. This goes to the core of the virtues that solicitors are expected to have. Although a dishonest solicitor might be an advantage to some clients, the rule of law would be quickly eroded if this is the norm. The SDT guidance notes on sanction state:

"A finding that an allegation of dishonesty has been proved will almost invariably lead to striking off, save in exceptional circumstances."[4]

The ultimate sanction is to strike a solicitor from the roll; this sanction applies only to the most serious breaches.

The guidance used by the SDT regarding dishonesty is:

"a standard which combines an objective and a subjective test, and which requires that before there can be a finding of dishonesty it must be established that the defendant's conduct was dishonest by the ordinary standards of reasonable and honest people and that he himself realised that by those standards his conduct was dishonest."

Whilst bad behaviour needs to be proven to the criminal standard at the SDT, the above is good guidance for solicitors to keep in mind in practice.

---

[4] *Twinsectra Ltd v Yardley & Ors [2002] UKHL 12*

We will also use examples from different practice areas that have come to our attention and look at the potential ethical issues that arise outside the most obvious and widely accepted examples above.

3.5   Duty to self-report

Every person regulated by the SRA has a duty to promptly self-report the following:

(a)   Serious financial difficulty;

(b)   Action taken against them by another regulator;

(c)   Serious failure to comply with or achieve the Principles, rules, Outcomes and other requirements of the Handbook.

Additionally, every person regulated by the SRA should:

(d)   Report any serious misconduct by any person or firm authorised by the SRA or any employee, manager or owner of any such firm.

This recognises the virtuous character of the solicitor - if you do something that you consider to be a "serious failure" then you should hand yourself in to the regulator. You cannot look the other way when it comes to your own failings or that of someone else within a regulated firm. This emphasises the duty to be positively ethical in the current era of outcomes-focused regulation. A solicitor's regulatory obligation is to self-govern and self-report - the regulator and public expect the highest standards.

Personal virtues or ethics are very important when making these decisions and we can see from decided SDT cases that there are solicitors who self-report their own failures. Members of the Bar have the same obligation to self-report, including serious professional misconduct.

> ### Scenario: Professional misconduct
>
> A criminal barrister unintentionally spoke to jurors after a trial in which he was involved. He apparently asked them about the basis for their verdict and disclosed to them that evidence was withheld from them. He received a fine of £300 and a reprimand. The panel took into account as mitigation that he had self-reported the matter and the fact that the conduct was unintentional.

It must have been extremely difficult for the barrister to make the admissions but the fact that he realised his mistake and promptly informed the regulator acted in his favour. His actions show that he was able to use his judgement to report the misconduct to the regulator. It is possible that the conversation would never have come to the attention of the regulator without the self-report. His action to self-report was ethically positive; he understood that he had done the wrong thing. The only way to put the matter right was to self-report and accept the consequences of his actions. Quite often in the SDT reports, solicitors who do one wrong thing and then attempt to cover up the initial error by doing a series of wrong things occasionally believe that they will be able to rectify the original error. This behaviour can lead to disastrous results.

In the SDT case below the Tribunal appreciated that it would be difficult for most people to self-report a conviction for a serious offence but that a solicitor should realise that self-reporting is essential, no matter what the consequences.

Scenario: Drink driving

Facts

Solicitor M pleaded guilty to a drink driving offence in 2013. It was her fourth offence and she was convicted of driving a motor vehicle with excess alcohol. She was also convicted of driving whilst disqualified from driving. She was driving without insurance and received a custodial sentence of 4 months which was suspended for 24 months.

She self-reported the conviction within 2 weeks of the sentence; her employer also reported the matter to the SRA.

Unfortunately, she did not self-report a conviction from 2011 but she had reported 2 earlier convictions for driving with excess alcohol in 1997 and 2000 which occurred prior to her admission to the roll.

Rules

It was alleged that she had breached Principles 1, 2 and 6.

Ethical issues/professional breaches

She was aware that the convictions needed to be reported but had failed to self-report the 2011 conviction.

She put forward mitigation regarding her personal circumstances but it was difficult for her to overcome the fact that it took over 2 years to report the 2011 conviction. She only admitted that conviction when asked a direct question by the SRA. In 2011 once her immediate personal difficulties had passed she didn't report.

The reason she gave the Tribunal for failing to report the conviction was the fact that she was convinced she would lose her job. Her decision-making was at that point in time based purely on self-interest. She was not immediately concerned with the Principles or the Code of Conduct.

Outcome

The Tribunal found that she had breached Principle 2 by failing to report the conviction.

The main concern of the Tribunal was to protect the reputation of the profession. In this case, the appropriate way to do so was to strike off the solicitor and order her to pay costs of £2,500.

In contrast to the barrister case above, this solicitor exacerbated her situation by failing to report the convictions in 2011. It should be noted that these incidents all occurred when the solicitor was not working; she was in her own time. None of the incidents involved a client but the number of incidents and the public nature of them were such that they were considered to be very serious.

3.6   Personal virtues

The virtues needed to guide a solicitor to act with integrity go some way towards understanding what it means to act with integrity; judgement, fairness and honesty are central. Additionally, we suggest that openness and transparency are key elements to acting with integrity.

When you are about to embark upon a course of action, whether in the work environment or outside it, it is useful to ask yourself what you would do if your mother/partner/children were watching you. This can sometimes alter the path that you might choose - the additional scrutiny of a close friend or family member can act to shame us out of making potentially unethical decisions.

In a more professional context, would you be able to justify your actions if you were cross-examined? How would you feel in the cold light of a courtroom if a judge scrutinised your decision?

This technique can be revealing about our ethical choices when you shine a light on them; taking a step back and then making a balanced decision can help to maintain integrity.

When are private emails not private?

In the following case, taken from the SDT decisions, 3 solicitors in the same firm sent each other emails that they didn't think would ever be seen by other people. One solicitor indicated that if he had known other people would read the emails he would never have written them and that in fact the content did not represent his views. The emails were sent between the 3 as a joke.

The 3 solicitors didn't stop to think about the content of the emails they were sending - they knew the emails weren't serious. The third respondent in his mitigation told the Tribunal that he *"shuddered to think he had been party to such emails; he was still struggling to understand how it was that he had written this material."*

Scenario: Rude emails

Facts

Solicitors A, B and C were all partners at the same firm. They were using the firm's email accounts to send each other emails that contained comments about co-workers that were described by the SDT as "crass, offensive, puerile and inappropriate." The solicitors did not think that anyone would ever read their emails aside from the recipients; a non-solicitor employee who revealed the content read them. She was the subject of some of the emails between the 3 partners. It is worth noting that;

- No clients were involved;
- No fraud was involved;
- No malice was intended;
- The solicitors didn't think anyone would ever see the emails.

Rules

Potential breach of Principles 2, 6 and 9 (not proven).

Potential ethical issues/professional breaches

The SDT found that the 3 solicitors had acted in a way that breached Principle 2 and Principle 6 - the requirement to act with integrity and not to behave in a way that diminishes the trust the public places in them or the legal profession.

This was to the criminal standard of proof. 2 solicitors were dismissed from the firm when the emails became known; the third had resigned before that time. All 3 were ashamed of what they had written.

The solicitors hadn't acted with integrity in that they weren't honest and open. They demonstrated a dire lack of judgement when sending the emails.

Solicitor A was fined £5,000 and costs of £2,700; Solicitor B was fined £5,000 and costs of £2,700; Solicitor C was fined £4,000 and costs of £1,800.

3.7   The ethical solicitor

For the purpose of this book, we are using a specific approach to ethical dilemmas and a specific definition of ethics. We therefore propose that a solicitor who behaves ethically is one who does so *even when no one is looking*. Take for example the barrister who self-reported his conversation with the jurors - it is possible that the BSB would never have come to find out about that matter unless he reported it. The solicitors who sent each other crass and offensive emails would have benefited from bearing this in mind when they sent them. They each believed that their emails were private and that no one would read them. Perhaps they would not have written the emails if they had approached the proposition thinking through the ethical issues. Perhaps the cynical solicitor will say that had they sent the emails from their personal email accounts instead of their firm accounts the outcome would have been different.

The issue of ethics isn't about what you do when you are likely to be scrutinised for your decision-making. It's about all those decisions you make in everyday life.

The ethical solicitor;

(1)   knows what the right thing is;

(2)   acts to do the right thing; and

(3)   does the right thing for the right reason,

even when no one is looking and no one is likely to find out what he/she has done.

Fig 15: Remember the motto for the ethical solicitor!

All professions are held in high regard in society because *"arguably professions were moral communities based upon shared expertise and occupational membership."*[5] The place of the professions in society is changing in the 21st century and some say that the regulation of these professions is not keeping pace with that change.

Scenario: Undercharged in a restaurant

Facts

You go to a restaurant and aren't charged for a bottle of wine you have ordered and drunk. Do you tell the waiter that there has been a mistake and pay the additional money? Or do you pay the bill and leave without mentioning it?

The process of ethical decision-making

Know the right thing - to pay for the wine you ordered.

Do the right thing - tell the waiter to add the wine to the bill.

---

[5] *In Professions We Trust (Phillip Blond, Elena Antonacopoulou and Adrian Pabst, July 2015)*

For the right reason - Principles 2 and 6; fairness, honesty, morality, good judgement.

The best ethical outcome is to pay for the wine. This may not be the best outcome for all parties at the table.

There are various other factors that might impact on the decision-making process:

Other people - your guests might not want to pay anything more than the original bill.

But you all drank the wine so its only fair that you all pay for it.

Money - you realise that you don't have enough money to pay for the wine. You only have enough to pay for your share of the original bill.

You could ask someone else to cover your share and pay them back at a later date.

Time - the restaurant is very busy and you need to get the last train home. You don't have time to wait for them to correct their mistake. If you wait, you'll have to get a taxi home and this will be very costly.

You could leave to catch your train and ask someone else to wait for the correct bill.

None of these other factors act to change the ethical decision; in fact, all they do is make it more difficult to make the **right** decision.

Many people would use the external factors as a justification not to make the right ethical decision. In fact, the above example shows that there are many ways around the other factors - if you look hard enough you should be able to make the right decision.

In the context of the solicitor's regulatory framework, what is "the right thing"? The SRA outlines that where one or more of the Principles clash *"the one which best serves the public interest in the particular circumstances, especially the public interest in the proper administration of justice"* should prevail.

Solicitors believe that they should act in the best interests of their client at all times. Where the solicitor works in-house or for influential individuals or companies, the temptation to place the interests of the clients above all else can be overwhelming. However, all solicitors must comply with the 10 Principles and the overarching obligation to ensure the proper administration of justice.

As in the examples above, there are times when the solicitor faces a dilemma that does not involve the client's interests at all. Principles 1, 2 and 6 are very important in times where client issues aren't the focus of the dilemma.

Ethics isn't *only* about compliance. We propose that every solicitor approaches every ethical issue from a compliance-based perspective *first*. As and when the Code of Conduct Outcomes require further thought, the next approach is from the point of view of the ethical solicitor. Remember the ethical solicitor's motto.

This decision-making process involves two traditional ethical approaches :

(1)   The rules-based approach - what does the SRA say we should do?

(2)   The virtuous approach - what would an ethical solicitor do?

The application of these two approaches will often result in a number of compliant solutions to the ethical dilemma; the individual solicitor then needs to decide which approach to take. The point at which a solicitor finds themselves with a variety of compliant options is when ethical issues are explored more deeply.

Taking this approach to ethical dilemmas both in and out of practice should help the solicitor when faced with sudden split second decision-making. Getting into the habit of ethical decision-making will make a difference in these situations. Consider the following case:

Scenario: Lying in court

Facts

Solicitor F gave evidence in court proceedings and he was asked in cross-examination whether, during the course of his career as a solicitor, any allegation or breach of the solicitors Code of Conduct had ever been upheld. He had answered no.

In fact he had been suspended from practice for two years from February 1995. His response was an automatic response, which was to tell a lie to end the cross-examination rather than tell the truth and face further questions.

4 months after giving oral evidence, he advised the solicitors for the Claimant that he had given incorrect information. The Claimant's solicitors reported his conduct to the SRA but they took no action at the time. It would be interesting to know why they didn't think that a solicitor lying in court needed further investigation.

Solicitor F self-reported to the SRA more than 2 years after the date that he gave the evidence. As a result of his self-report the matter was referred to the SDT.

Rules/ethical issues

Technically his answer on cross-examination had been the truth but he knew that the question was a broad question, which wasn't specifically about this conduct under the Code of Conduct 2007 which was in place at that time. The reasons for his previous suspension were in respect of accounts rules breaches and conduct unbefitting of a solicitor.

The Tribunal stated: "Ordinary members of the public would expect a solicitor to be frank, transparent and complete in the giving of evidence." Solicitor F had not been frank and honest with the court.

Outcome

Solicitor F was fined £10,000 and ordered to pay costs of £6,000.

Had Solicitor F developed the habit of ethical decision-making, he may not have lied in court despite the difficult position he found himself in at that time.

3.8   Identify the ethical dilemma

Real life ethical dilemmas aren't often very straightforward. There are often a number of external factors that the solicitor needs to take into account when reaching a decision. It can be a problem for an individual solicitor to identify the fact that the issue at hand is in fact an *ethical* dilemma in the first place. The first step is to identify the problem, recognise the ethical issues and then act accordingly.

Scenario: Tampering with forms

Facts

A solicitor sees a client and asks him to complete and sign a form to send to the Legal Aid Agency. When the client leaves the office, the solicitor realises that the client forgot to complete his address on the form.

What is the right thing to do?

There could be a number of possible options to explore:

Option A: The solicitor completes the address and submits the form - after all no one will ever find out.

Option B: The solicitor completes the address and submits the form with the amendment initialled by the solicitor, thereby ensuring that the recipient knows there has been an amendment.

Option C: The solicitor speaks to the client and asks them if they have the authority to change the form to add in the address. The solicitor keeps an attendance note of the conversation.

Option D: The solicitor asks the client to return to the office to complete the address (and initial the amendment).

What does the solicitor do?

The first consideration should be with reference to the SRA Principles and Code of Conduct with an eye on the prospect of any sanction. This is known as a rules-based approach, but the decision-making process doesn't end there. Once any obviously non-compliant options have been ruled out, the solicitor could choose any of the remaining options.

Many solicitors reading this will know instantly what choice they would make and this is likely to reveal much about the individual's virtues and ethics.

SRA Principles/outcomes to consider - the rules-based approach

Principle 2: Act with integrity.

Principle 5: Provide a proper standard of service to your clients.

Principle 6: Behave in a way that maintains the trust the public places in you and the provision of legal services.

Outcome (11.1): Do not take unfair advantage of third parties in your personal or professional capacity.

Act with integrity

Some solicitors may think that it is perfectly fine to change something as uncontentious as a client's address and opt for Option A above on the basis that "no one will ever know" or "what harm can be done by adding in a simple address?"

Others will think that it is unacceptable to change anything on a form signed by a client and ask the client to return to amend the form (Option D above).

Bear in mind the personal characteristics for the ideal lawyer - honesty, fairness, openness and transparency.

SRA approach

When we presented the SRA ethics team with this scenario they advised us to take Option D.

Documents should never be presented as having been signed by the client unless that is the case. Even minor changes are unacceptable.

However, when pushed, the SRA ethics adviser conceded that Option C may be acceptable as long as the third party is aware of who inserted the details of the address. Options A and B are not likely to keep the regulator happy.

The ethical solicitor

As the regulatory approach discounts Options A and B the ethical solicitor has two remaining choices, Options C or D. This is therefore a dilemma that has an ethical element, albeit quite subtle.

If you are doing the right thing for the right reason, the focus has to be client-based in the context of the regulatory framework. This is where the solicitor's action needs to be context specific. For example, if there is no major inconvenience to the client to return to sign the document then that is the approach to take.

If the client is unable to return, refuses to return, or suffers a disability that prevents them from returning the solicitor will need to consider whether it is appropriate to take the form to the client to complete the address details.

Only in limited specific circumstances could it possibly be necessary to alter the document on behalf of the client.

Other considerations

The Legal Aid Agency could reject the amended application and require the client to complete the form.

This will then cause delay, which might not be in the best interests of the client.

Different facts - different result?

What if we propose to change the details of a will rather than a legal aid form?

Your answer may change depending on the nature of the document but the answer is likely to be the same no matter what the document is.

By approaching all ethical dilemmas in the above way, you should reach the same result.

Solicitors would agree that it is unacceptable to change any aspect of the will after the client has signed it.

3.9   Do <u>you</u> need to learn how to behave ethically?

Many solicitors think that this is "someone else's problem"; <u>you</u> don't need to read this book or go on a course to learn how to behave ethically. In fact, many people don't think it is possible to teach virtuous behaviour; this is something innate or learned earlier in life.

You may know someone in your office who could do with a "steer" in the right direction. When solicitors talk about ethical breaches, often they are recounting someone else's poor choices - rarely are they admitting to their own transgressions.

It's not you; it's them.

This type of thinking isn't unusual. Older practitioners possibly think that younger solicitors need more ethics grounding because they are "wet behind the ears" or too inexperienced to have sound judgement to make the "right decisions". As we will see using our examples, there can often be more than one option which leads to a compliant result; the ethical measure of the response is down to the individual to some extent.

Younger practitioners may believe that older practitioners need more ethics grounding because they have been practicing law for too long. Rather than this having a positive impact on the ethics of a practitioner it can conversely be seen to be detrimental. The older practitioner can pick up bad habits; the same could be said for older drivers. Both pick up bad habits that go undetected until an "impact event", when something goes hideously wrong and then the bad practices have a light shone on them.

In the SDT decisions there is often a distinction made between the older experienced practitioner and the younger "foolish" solicitor. That is not to say that a younger solicitor will not receive the same sanction as an older solicitor for the same breach but it is clear in mitigation that age is a factor that is taken into account. The UCL Report of Professional Standards indicates that competence of the solicitor impacted on the level of seriousness perceived by those taking the survey. In one example, a newly qualified solicitor's error is treated more leniently when compared to a similar problem in which the solicitor was not identified as newly qualified; this may be reflected in SDT decisions although there is no research to support this.

One possible reason that different generations of solicitors could regard each other as being in need of ethics grounding is that they have learned different systems of regulation.

3.10 What is the right thing?

When thinking through a practical/ethical dilemma, there are various parties who are directly or indirectly involved in the solicitor's decision-making process.

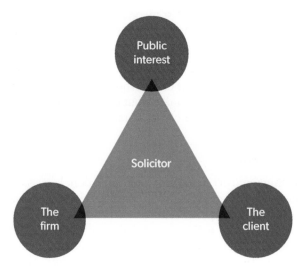

Fig 16: The solicitor isn't making decisions in isolation to other people!

Public interest is at the pinnacle of the triangle because the regulatory Principles and Code indicate that solicitors should balance their obligations under the Principles and Code to protect the administration of justice for the public interest. This means that no individual's interests rank in priority over this obligation.

In real life, if a solicitor faces a practical/ethical dilemma, the answer isn't as straightforward as looking it up in the rules. The solicitor needs to keep an eye on the regulatory objectives but also weigh the firm's commercial interests and the public interest too.

Scenario: Double billing

Facts

You travel from London to Leeds to have a meeting with client A at their request. You prepare for the meeting in the office charging the client for the preparation time. The journey to Leeds is just over 2 hours and you decide to work on client B's file during the journey. How do you bill the journey time?

- Do you bill client A for the journey time and client B for the work done during the journey, thus effectively double billing?
- Or do you bill client B for the preparation work but don't charge client A at all?

Clients A and B might not be too happy to be told that they were both charged for the same 2 hour period, even though you were effectively working for them both during that period.

Regulatory matters

Principle 2: Act with integrity.

Principle 4: Act in the best interests of each client.

Principle 6: Behave in a way that maintains the trust the public places in you and in the provision of legal services.

Outcome (1.12): Clients are in a position to make informed decisions about the services they need, how their matter will be handled and the options available to them.

Outcome (1.13): Clients receive the best possible information, both at the time of engagement and when appropriate as their matter progresses, about the likely overall cost of their matter.

There is no rule that prevents a solicitor from charging twice for the same time. Many firms would think that this is an efficient use of time.

Potential ethical issues

The public might not think that it is "ethical" or fair for both clients A and B to be charged for the same time.

Your firm/department/immediate supervisor may think it is entirely appropriate for you to bill both clients at your full hourly rate for the work done on the train.

This may clash with the individual solicitor's desire to bill only client B for the work as being an individual ethical decision. The firm's influence is usually commercially led and takes priority over the individual solicitor's ethical compass.

The fact that you haven't told either client that you are charging them both for the same time isn't likely to be compliant. Neither does it show a high level of integrity, if integrity is synonymous with transparency and fairness.

There isn't one right answer but a range of answers that could be considered to be acceptable within the current regulatory framework. Openness and transparency are key in dealing with this type of dilemma.

3.11 Do the right thing

This seems to be easy to say but difficult to do. Often the external influences disrupt the solicitor from doing the right thing or can cause the solicitor to do something unethical.

When it comes to doing the right thing, dozens of SDT cases evidence the fact that many solicitors don't manage to do the right thing, even though they usually know what they should have done. When a case comes before the SDT, it means that the individual solicitor has been caught doing the wrong thing and that there may even be criminal charges against that individual.

In practice, solicitors all do something that could be considered to be unethical. Even when a solicitor is committing an unethical act, it is highly likely that they know that they are doing the wrong thing.

The question has to be that if the "ethical solicitor" knows what the right thing is, why don't they do it? The transgressions of the solicitors reported in the SDT case reports seem obviously unethical; of course, a solicitor shouldn't reveal the identity of their client to anyone else, but it happens.

Scenario: Confidentiality

Facts

A solicitor leaked information about the true identity of the author Robert Galbraith, thereby breaching the author's confidentiality. The solicitor told his wife's best friend during a private conversation. The information then appeared in a national newspaper.

Outcome

The SRA rebuked the solicitor and ordered him to pay a fine of £1,000.

The author brought a legal action against the firm who made an undisclosed donation to a charity in settlement.

External influences somehow outweigh the solicitor's correct ethical judgement, for various reasons. Many of you will think that this is just the way of the world and accept this as a risk of being in practice, whether in private practice or in-house. However, if we accept that the ethical solicitor knows what the right thing is and then acts upon that knowledge, external influences should have no impact on the decision-making process. Many of you will reject this notion entirely as being unrepresentative of your experience in the practice of law. It seems to be totally alien to your direct experiences but the cases from the SDT show that the Tribunal expects all solicitors, including trainees, to do the right thing regardless of external influences.

Potential external influences on the ethical decision-making process

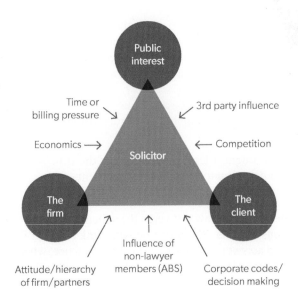

Fig 17: How does the solicitor do the right thing with external issues that need to be balanced?

3.12 The firm's influence on the "ethical solicitor"

Bad apple, bad barrel or bad orchard?

Sometimes the culture of the firm is such that the decision-making process-es don't operate the way they should. This could be because one influential person is influencing another's decision-making processes to suit their own needs. In these cases it could be the case of a bad apple - one person who is affecting other solicitors. Or it could be a bad barrel - a certain team or department are operating unethically and because that behaviour is encouraged or accepted the members of that team don't recognise that what they are doing is unethical. In the worst cases, which would be rare, the firm or that particular sector is so competitive that the expectation is that everyone will conduct themselves in the same, unethical, way.

The following phrases aren't uncommon to hear from solicitors regarding ethical decision-making:

- "Solicitor X does whatever s/he wants to do and gets away with it" - *Bad apple?*

- "If it was up to me I would do Y but solicitor X told me to do Z" - *Bad barrel?*

- "If I make the right (ethical) decision, I will lose my job and if people find out what I did I won't get a job in this sector again" - *Bad orchard?*

The individual solicitor may perceive that there is an unethical culture in the firm for some reason and use that belief as a reason for justifying their own unethical decision-making.

Remember that "the ethical solicitor" makes ethical choices no matter what external pressure may be applied by third parties for the wrong reasons.

Hierarchy

It is inevitable that the internal hierarchy of a private firm will influence the independence of every solicitor working in that firm. For those solicitors working in-house this problem becomes increasingly more difficult as there is only one client and the solicitor will not be able to walk away from that client without losing their job.

Independence within the firm

Principle 3 states that a solicitor should not allow their independence to be compromised; this is often associated with external influences on a solicitor.

However, the notion of independence is difficult to achieve in the context of power distribution within a firm. It is expected that "the ethical solicitor" won't be influenced by external factors. Arguably, many firms wouldn't want these types of solicitors to be recruited - many firms only recruit from within so that they can build the culture they want within a firm. External hires can upset the apple cart if the culture of the previous firm clashes with that of the new employer. In the case of takeovers, the problem can be exacerbated with the culture of one firm clashing with that of the other. The employees of the firm that is taken over could view the culture of the new firm as "bad barrel" or "bad orchard" scenarios causing an ethical ticking time bomb.

Fig 18: The ethical moral compass might be stronger or weaker in different solicitors

It is easy to see from this model that the number of years a solicitor has practised and their standing within the firm will impact on their ability to influence other solicitors and their ethical behaviour. Most fee earners will also be able to influence the other staff to a varying degree; it isn't unheard of for secretaries, paralegals and administrative staff to be asked to do something that would constitute both an ethical and compliance issue for a solicitor. Whilst the non-solicitor staff aren't shown on the above model, it is easy to imagine that paralegals, secretaries and other support staff sit at the weak end of the arrow. Likewise non-legal managers of ABSs sit at the strong end and it is known that their non-legal influence on the structure of the firm is very great.

It is difficult to introduce successful ethics training programmes within a firm unless those solicitors (or non-legal managers) with the most influence participate and also act in ethical ways. The approach of the most influential members will impact the daily running of the firm. Any training must start with that of the people who have a strong influence and they must inject ethics training at a grassroots level.

3.13   Is unethical behaviour deeply embedded at your firm?

Fig 19: Is there one person causing ethical issues within the firm or is it the firm or sector that is infected with poor ethical decision-making?

Scenario: Pressure on junior solicitor

Facts

Solicitor S is 2 years PQE having trained and qualified with a Tier 1 Legal 500 firm - referred to as a "silver circle" firm.

S/he is told by a Partner to telephone a client to tell the client (in a roundabout way) to find, sign and backdate a vital document.

It seems that the Partner didn't get the vital document signed at the right time during a transaction and this will have a huge tax implication for the client. It is in the client's best interests to have the document in their possession.

Regulatory position

The junior solicitor must observe the following Principles when deciding what action to take:

Principle 1: Uphold the rule of law and proper administration of justice.

Principle 2: Act with integrity.

Principle 3: Do not allow your independence to be compromised.

Principle 6: Behave in a way that maintains the trust the public places in you and in the provision of legal services.

Outcome (1.1): You treat your clients fairly.

Outcome (1.16): You inform current clients if you discover any act or omission which could give rise to a claim by them against you.

Outcome (11.1): You do not take unfair advantage of third parties in either your professional or personal capacity (in this context HMRC who will lose tax as a result of backdating the document).

What does the junior solicitor do?

Option A: Do what the Partner says and hope that there is no regulatory fallout.

Option B: Go over the Partner's head and report the problem to the ethics department at the firm or a more senior person in the hope that they will broker a sensible resolution.

Option C: Report the breach to the COLP at the firm in the hope that s/he will broker a sensible resolution.

Option D: Tell the client that they might have a claim against the firm due to the Partner's error.

Option E: Speak to the Partner about the ethical issues and discuss the difficult position the junior solicitor is in as a result of the Partner's direction.

Potential ethical issues

The junior solicitor is culpable for his/her decision. The fact that the decision was directed by a more senior solicitor doesn't override the individual's responsibility to the client.

Option A isn't an ethical solution to the problem because it is doing the wrong thing for the wrong reason (protecting the Partner/protecting the firm).

Options B to E are all ethical solutions as they could all lead to the client being informed about the negligent action of the Partner who failed to get a signature on a vital document.

The junior solicitor may not know if the problem is:

- a bad apple - the Partner is acting without the knowledge or consent of the firm;
- a bad barrel - the department or firm condones/encourages this behaviour and internal reporting won't do any good;
- a bad orchard - this type of behaviour is commonplace in this sector/firm (which still doesn't excuse the behaviour).

The junior solicitor therefore doesn't know how to approach the dilemma which could be as follows:

- Bad apple - Choose Option B or E;
- Bad barrel - Choose Option C, D or E;
- Bad orchard - Choose Option D (but more likely to choose Option A if the junior solicitor feels there will be no action if they report further up the line).

A junior solicitor could struggle with Option E whereas a more senior solicitor in that position might always start with that option.

The ethical solicitor

The ethical solicitor knows what the right thing is and does the right thing, for the right reason. Although it is in the client's best interests to have the document signed, it isn't acting with integrity to falsify documents to achieve that end. It could be said that by taking option D the solicitor is acting in the best interests of the client in the most ethical way. Being transparent about the issue and alerting the client to potential claims that can be made could be seen to be the most ethical solution.

- The right thing to do - don't sign the document.
- Acting on that knowledge - Options B, C, D, E.
- For the right reason - to protect the client's interests (not cover up the Partner's wrong doing).

In the following case, the SDT dealt with an individual solicitor who outlined a firm where unethical practices were widely practised. Solicitors shared tips with each other to circumvent the firm's file checking systems to ensure that files were active. This seems to be a bad barrel situation.

Scenario: Fabricating documents

Facts

Solicitor L was accused of fabricating documents to cover up in-activity on her files. By doing so she misled the client and the firm about the progress she was making.

Rules

Principle 2: Act with integrity.

Principle 4: Act in the best interests of each client.

Principle 5: Provide a proper standard of service to your clients.

Principle 6: Behave in a way that maintains the trust the public places in you and in the provision of legal services.

Ethical issues/professional breaches

Many difficulties for this solicitor came from the fact that she was covering up the actions of the Partner at a branch office. The Partner would often be absent from the office, working from home or a flat in Scotland. He would leave instructions that the other Partners were not to be told he was not there. This type of behaviour creates an unstable work environment and in this case for Solicitor L working unsupervised and under pressure.

The Partner told Solicitor L that she would be made redundant if she didn't meet her targets. He also told her that if she complained to the other Partners the department would be closed.

Another solicitor at the firm showed Solicitor L how to alter time recording to avoid the supervisor from finding out about delay on her files. This practice was widespread amongst the fee earners at the firm. This seems to indicate that the barrel was bad, perhaps as a result of the Partner's actions.

Outcome

Whilst the solicitor made the wrong choices for which she was suspended indefinitely, there are other interesting matters.

Possible approaches

In hindsight, Solicitor L told the SDT that she wished she had approached another Partner at the other office who she thought would have helped her.

The COLP should have been the first port of call.

3.14 Do the right thing - for the right reason

Solicitors are undoubtedly influenced by third parties and external factors to act with the wrong reason in mind. For example:

(a)   The solicitor wants to protect themselves against a complaint;

(b)   The solicitor is being asked to cover up a mistake for someone else;

(c)   The solicitor is protecting a senior solicitor against a complaint, criminal or civil action;

(d)   The solicitor is protecting the reputation of the firm;

(e)   The solicitor is maximising profit;

(f)   The solicitor is maximising billable hours;

(g)   The solicitor is protecting his or her job;

(h)   Other financial or managerial concerns.

Any solicitor who acts with these goals in mind isn't acting in an ethical way, although many of you will recognise that it is very easy to put personal or firm interests above those of the individual client or the Principles laid out by the SRA.

In the above example, Solicitor L acted in a way to protect the Partner who was absent from the office without informing the other Partners. She covered up his wrongdoing but by doing so she started to commit her own wrongdoings.

Occasionally the solicitor believes they are doing the right thing to protect the client but by doing so they breach other codes of conduct. For example, a solicitor who covered up the fact that an Employment Tribunal case had been dismissed thought they were protecting the client by doing this but of course the solicitor lied to the client repeatedly.

3.15 Conclusion

Each solicitor will decide for themselves during the course of their practice which end of the ethical scale they choose to practise. What is certain is that there is no definite ethical line that we can all agree on.

Ethical | Unethical

There are multiple shades of grey and we need to find a shade that we are comfortable with after careful consideration of the regulatory framework.

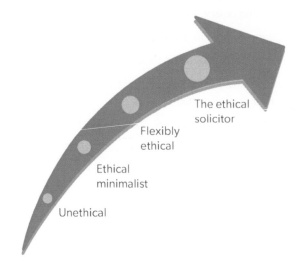

Fig 20: What is your position with regard to risk within the regulatory framework?

Sometimes the choices you make are dictated by the area of law you choose to specialise in; tax law and family law will bring their own unique challenges. The choices you make within your subject area will also be affected by the ethical behaviour of our peers, the Partners and more increasingly the non-lawyers. Whether they are managers in an ABS or corporate leaders in industry, they wield a lot of power. One matter that all solicitors must be aware of is the fact that ultimately you make your own choices. You decide how to act along the ethical scale and only you will be held responsible for those decisions.

Hopefully, the SDT cases we use in this chapter highlight that many of the "wrong" choices are made when solicitors aren't thinking about consequences or ethics at all. The example of the solicitors who sent crass emails thinking that no one would ever see them is the perfect case in point. In much the same way that learner drivers are taught to "mirror, signal, manoeuvre" until the repeated action becomes second nature, we propose that solicitors should learn to:

Think twice, act once

Fig 21: The old carpenter's proverb works here with a little adaptation - rather than "measure twice, cut once" we say that "think twice, act once" will have the same affect!

Many solicitors don't believe that they need to bother with "ethics" - they know the difference between right and wrong. Many solicitors are able to practise without ever attracting the notice of the SRA, which doesn't mean that they are supremely ethical or ethically minimalist. Solicitors in the 21st century need to ensure that they are familiar with the current system of regulation and how modern practices exert pressure over solicitors that can lead to unethical behaviour.

Behaving unethically can be a bit like 'flu in the sense that it can be catching. What was once a bad apple can infect the whole barrel. A solicitor who implements the "think twice, act once" methodology is not only setting a template for himself or herself but also setting standards for others. What might seem to some as being unnecessary behaviour could impact the culture of the firm in a positive way.

Chapter 4: The client is king

4.1   Introduction

The relationship between the solicitor and their client is very important - the client needs the expertise of the solicitor and often that means that the solicitor is in a position of power and control. The relationship with the client is not the only relationship that needs to be monitored - often it isn't even the most important relationship the solicitor has. In Chapter 3 we explored the different obligations a solicitor has to the public in general as well as to the client. It is important that the client maintains their personal integrity at all times and honours their obligation to uphold the rule of law and the proper administration of justice. The client may not realise how broad the solicitor's obligations are when they retain their services.

The man on the Clapham omnibus may not know that buying a solicitor's time is different to buying a mechanic's time, for example. After all, if you took your car to a mechanic to repair the brakes, you wouldn't expect the mechanic to refuse because they have ethical objections to the way you drive your car. In the same way, the average client wouldn't expect a solicitor to refuse to represent them in a criminal case after telling the solicitor that they are guilty. The regulatory and ethical factors that interact with the client relationship are complex.

As expected there is a panoply of obligations set out by the SRA that regulate how solicitors should treat their clients and this applies whether the client is a regular user of legal services or a novice. We may see a shift in the number of mandatory Outcomes in the next edition of the Code of Conduct; this would be in keeping with Outcomes-Focused Regulation. Many of the current rules that regulate the client relationship are in connection with the deployment of client funds but this is outside the scope of this text. The Solicitors' Accounts Rules remain mainly rules-based for the protection of client assets and so the ethical obligations are clearly set out.

The Outcomes exist to ensure that the client is protected and informed of their rights. In theory this should mean that the client should not have any need to complain about the service received. However, complaints are inevitable - statistics produced by the Legal Ombudsman (LeO) show that commercial clients rarely complain to them about the service they receive. Many more complaints arise from clients requiring personal advice; these clients tend to be irregular users of legal services, whose expectations may not be met by their first interaction with legal service providers. It is useful to understand what is regulated behaviour, why it is regulated and what clients complain about. We deal with the complaints aspects of client service in detail in Chapter 6: Complaints and negligence.

Over the last 5 years the highest number of complaints dealt with by the LeO have been about residential conveyancing - 23% in the year 2014/2015. Contrast this with complaints about commercial conveyancing where complaints have been less than 1%. LeO on average accepts 7,500 cases per annum which means that on average 1,725 of those are about residential conveyancing. This either indicates that commercial clients don't make complaints or that their complaints are resolved by the firm without the need for LeO to get involved.

4.2 Regulatory issues

We looked at the 10 Principles and the ethical elements of each in Chapter 2: Rules-based ethics so we do not propose to duplicate that commentary here. It is instructive to take a close look at the Code of Conduct to see what the regulatory starting point is.

Issues about client care are set out in Chapter 1 of the Code of Conduct and many of them are there to ensure that clients are protected and informed about their rights when dealing with a solicitor. Due to the power imbalance between the solicitor providing personal services and the client, it is important that these safety checks are kept in place. However, commercial clients may not benefit from any additional protections by the existence of these regulations. Further, it would be difficult to see how these apply directly to an in-house solicitor who typically will have only one client. A complaint that is regularly voiced is that the SRA Principles and Code of Conduct do not provide a framework that is suitable for all types of practitioner.

4.3 Outcomes

Some of the mandatory Outcomes are prescriptive, rules-based requirements and others have ethical dimensions. The table below sets out which category each of the Outcomes falls into.

Outcome	Rules-based	Ethical basis
O(1.1): you treat your clients fairly		✓
O(1.2): you provide services to your clients in a manner which protects their interests in their matter, subject to the proper administration of justice		✓
O(1.3): when deciding whether to act, or terminate your instructions, you comply with the law and the Code	✓	

Outcome	Rules-based	Ethical basis
O(1.4): you have the resources, skills and procedures to carry out your clients' instructions	✓	
O(1.5): the service you provide to clients is competent, delivered in a timely manner and takes account of your clients' needs and circumstances		✓
O(1.6): you only enter into fee agreements with your clients that are legal, and which you consider are suitable for the client's needs and take account of the client's best interests	✓	✓
O(1.7): you inform clients whether and how the services you provide are regulated and how this affects the protections available to the client	✓	
O(1.8): clients have the benefit of your compulsory professional indemnity insurance and you do not exclude or attempt to exclude liability below the minimum level of cover required by the SRA Indemnity Insurance Rules	✓	
O(1.9): clients are informed in writing at the outset of their matter of their right to complain and how complaints can be made	✓	
O(1.10): clients are informed in writing, both at the time of engagement and at the conclusion of your complaints procedure, of their right to complain to the Legal Ombudsman, the time frame for doing so and full details of how to contact the Legal Ombudsman	✓	
O(1.11): clients' complaints are dealt with promptly, fairly, openly and effectively		✓

Outcome	Rules-based	Ethical basis
O(1.12): clients are in a position to make informed decisions about the services they need, how their matter will be handled and the options available to them	✓	
O(1.13): clients receive the best possible information, both at the time of engagement and when appropriate as their matter progresses, about the likely overall cost of their matter	✓	
O(1.14): clients are informed of their right to challenge or complain about your bill and the circumstances in which they may be liable to pay interest on an unpaid bill	✓	
O(1.15): you properly account to clients for any financial benefit you receive as a result of your instructions	✓	
O(1.16): you inform current clients if you discover any act or omission which could give rise to a claim by them against you	✓	✓

We will explore the ethical dimensions of those Outcomes identified above. Complaints are dealt with in Chapter 6 so we will not mention them here.

Outcome (1.1): You treat your clients fairly

The possible ethical dimensions to this Outcome are plentiful; the concept of fairness is quite subjective even when taken in the context of this regulatory structure. There is little guidance in the Indicative Behaviours that would evidence that a client has been treated fairly.

Fairness is defined as follows:

(1) The ability to make judgements free from discrimination or dishonesty; this would be a "value ethics" definition. Using your personal values can you treat this client "fairly"?

(2) The conformity with rules or standards. This is a "rules-based" approach to problem solving - what do the rules and regulations say about the matter? Once you can answer that question you have your answer - there are few grey areas with this type of regulation.

This Outcome operates in conjunction with Principle 4 that requires the solicitor to act in the best interests of each client. The client is entitled to expect that you will act with integrity towards them and to do what is in their best interests. However, this is not a carte blanche to disregard the instructions of the client. There can often be a strain between what you believe to be in the best interests of your client and what they believe to be in their best interests. We look at this further in Chapter 8 which explores the use of litigation and ADR.

Outcome (1.2): You provide services to your clients in a manner which protects their interests in their matter, subject to the proper administration of justice

This Outcome highlights the inevitable tension between the client's instructions and the legality of doing what they want you to do. The rather basic example given in the introduction to this chapter is that of the criminal defence solicitor. Imagine that the solicitor attends a police station to be informed by the client that they did commit the crime that they are accused of. However, they instruct the solicitor to help them fabricate a believable alternate version of events. This behaviour does not uphold the proper administration of justice.

Scenario: Helping someone to avoid arrest

Facts

A criminal solicitor informed a client that the police were looking to arrest him and gave him some advice on how to leave the country. He suggested to the client that there were a couple of routes that he could take, one of which was via Dublin. The police wrongly believed that the client was already in prison on other offences when in fact he had been released on home detention which is how he had avoided arrest to that point.

Rules

Principle 1: Whilst this might satisfy the requirement to protect a client's interest it certainly doesn't uphold the rule of law and the administration of justice.

Principle 2: Act with integrity. Many would agree that the solicitor wasn't acting with integrity when he alerted his client about his potential arrest. The local press reported that he was the "go-to-guy" for some of the area's most notorious criminals. Perhaps not the reputation that most solicitors would seek to foster.

Principle 3: Do not allow your independence to be compromised. Arguably the solicitor hasn't acted in an independent way - he has acted favourably towards the client for some reason.

Principle 6: Behave in a way that maintains the trust the public places in him. The public would not expect solicitors to aid a criminal in his escape from arrest.

Breaches

The solicitor in question was heard on a listening device monitored by the police giving the advice to the client who almost managed to escape the country. He was imprisoned for 2 years for perverting the course of justice and struck off by the SRA.

All the regulatory breaches were made out against him in his absence. It is interesting to note that the solicitor had not accepted that he had perverted the course of justice by warning his client to flee.

The remarks of the sentencing judge assisted the Tribunal in the absence of the solicitor who failed to engage with the process;

> "...it is abundantly clear to me that by last year you had completely lost your moral compass and instead of seeking to uphold the course of justice you were doing what you could to assist to pervert it.
>
> ...There is no higher degree of trust than [sic] can be placed upon anybody than as being an officer of the court and the system of justice places that highest degree of trust in you as a solicitor."

The solicitor was ordered to pay costs of £3,350.

Outcome (1.5): The service you provide to clients is competent, delivered in a timely manner and takes account of your clients' needs and circumstances

Parts of this Outcome depend on adherence to rules - for example delivering service in a timely manner will not have an ethical element, per se. Clients' complaints that a matter took too long to complete, when there was no specified period within which completion was required to take place, are common.

Whether a solicitor is competent or not is a matter that we explored a little further when looking at Principle 5 in Chapter 2: Rules-based ethics.

However, this Outcome requires the solicitor to take into account the client's needs and circumstances. This can be difficult when dealing with vulnerable clients and those with fluid capacity. In these instances, the solicitor has to engage additional protection for the client to ensure that the client understands the advice that is being given and that their circumstances are assessed regularly.

This can be tricky where the client doesn't disclose any special needs but it becomes clear during the course of the retainer that there might be issues that the solicitor needs to work with. For example, some clients may not admit that they can't read, are dyslexic, deaf, etc. Where the client has suffered a bereavement or is in the process of getting divorced, client service needs to be adjusted to take these factors into account.

IB(1.6) states that in taking instructions and during the course of the retainer, solicitors should have proper regard to their client's mental capacity or other vulnerability, such as incapacity or duress. These issues are relevant to personal service retainers but may not be at all relevant for in-house solicitors.

The Law Society issued a practice note in 2015 giving guidance on how to meet the needs of vulnerable clients. The Law Society highlights the difficulty for vulnerable clients to access legal services. Solicitors should adapt their practices to identify those clients and adapt their practice to meet their client's needs. Three categories of vulnerable client are identified;

- Clients who have capacity to give instructions but due to a range of physical or mental disabilities need enhanced support from the solicitor to give instructions;

- Clients who lack mental capacity to make decisions;

- Clients who are vulnerable to undue influence or duress who may or may not have mental capacity to make decisions and give instructions.

All solicitors should understand these differences and assess clients who may be vulnerable so that they can adapt their practice to meet the needs of that client.

Scenario: Inappropriate dealings with the client

Facts

A married family solicitor was acting for a vulnerable victim of domestic abuse. During this difficult time he sent her inappropriate text messages which were characterised as "flirtatious". He was representing the woman in a domestic violence application.

During the period of 9 days he referred to her ex-boyfriend as a "cheeky tw*t" and sent multiple messages telling her that she was "lovely" and a "right glamour puss". He invited her out to lunch which she believed to be an invitation to a date. She had responded to the text messages at the time in a similar way.

Rules

Principle 4: Act in the best interests of each client;

Principle 6: Behave in a way that maintains the trust the public places in him.

Breaches

He was dismissed by his firm when his messages came to light and he had not been able to find work in the profession afterwards.

The client told the SDT that the messages made her sick and she felt that she had no choice but to respond to the messages because she did not want to jeopardise her case. This is a classic example of the power imbalance between a solicitor and client, which is highlighted when the client is vulnerable. There were many text and WhatsApp messages between the solicitor and the client and many of them referred to her physical appearance. She had also complained that her solicitor had hugged her and held her hands at least once.

Some allegations regarding the text messages were proven to the required standard; he was found to be in breach of Principles 4 and 6 and Outcome (1.1) - to treat clients fairly.

Only one of the numerous allegations had been proven against the solicitor and he was fined £5,000, which was more than just a nominal order to register the Tribunal's disapproval of the solicitor's conduct. Costs were ordered against him of £3,500.

Suggested course of action

The Tribunal recommended that the majority of allegations were not proven to the required standard, and some sound advice was given for other solicitors to bear in mind:

> *"This case demonstrated the need for solicitors to avoid any dealings with clients which were or could be viewed as inappropriate.*

> *Solicitors ought generally to avoid the use of bad language unless it was clearly necessary.... Solicitors should also beware of patronising clients by suggesting there was any need to "go down" to their level. Whilst many clients might benefit from being treated in a friendly and informal way others, including victims of domestic violence, might benefit more from being treated respectfully."*

Outcome (1.16): You inform current clients if you discover any act or omission which could give rise to a claim by them against you

This Outcome represents the essence of what virtue ethics is about. The "ethical solicitor" is honest enough to recognise when they have done something which could lead to a claim being made, they recognise that they have a duty to "do the right thing" and report the error or oversight to the client. It is difficult to say how many solicitors are able to recognise such a failing on their own part. There are instances in the SDT cases of solicitors self-reporting issues which are not proceeded with by the SRA only for the matter to be treated quite seriously by the Tribunal.

There is a similar regulatory requirement for firms to self-report major compliance breaches and the SRA believes that this has led to greater compliance within firms. This is similar to the way in which the financial services sector approaches regulation, nominating a compliance officer to ensure adherence to the FCA regulations.

Since the introduction of compliance officers in firms, self-reporting incidents to the SRA have rocketed. Many of these reports involve the misappropriation of funds either by partners or bookkeepers.

The SRA has a number of case studies on its website which demonstrate some reports received from compliance officers - they can be summarised as follows:

(1)   A secretary in the wills and probate department approached a client who had received an inheritance with an investment opportunity. The client was not sophisticated, and also vulnerable with the recent bereavement. The secretary was dismissed. The SRA is investigating.

(2)   A COLP reported to the SRA that the firm had not registered with the Information Commissioner. There was no evidence of detriment to clients during the short period that the firm was not registered. The breach was not material and did not need to be made.

(3)   During the administration of an estate, the solicitor had on 6 occasions transferred money from office to client account for the

payment of costs totalling £36,956. No invoices were raised and the beneficiaries were not notified of the costs. These are material breaches but the matter had been rectified.

The SRA doesn't seem to have any statistics available on their website that indicates how many self-reports are made under this requirement.

4.4 In-house practice

Different types of clients require different treatment. Many of the Outcomes we have looked at would have different applicability to corporate or in-house clients. One of the reasons that the SRA is about to introduce two separate Codes of Conduct is so that all solicitors are held to the same Code of Conduct whether they work in-house or not. These roles present new and diverse ethical issues. This is a topical issue with recent reports highlighting the challenges that face in-house counsel. The number of lawyers employed in an in-house capacity has increased over the years and their role is constantly changing. It is estimated that between the years 2000 and 2012 the number of solicitors working in-house doubled and this trend is set to continue. By 2015, 21.6% of all practising solicitors were working in-house.

It seems to be increasingly recognised that in-house lawyers are facing an ethical minefield with obligations to uphold the rule of law straining against acting in the best interests of their client, the employer.

The difficult balance that in-house solicitors must tackle is that between acting in the client's best interests and ensuring that they maintain their duty to act with integrity, to uphold the rule of law and the proper administration of justice.

In private practice for firms offering mainly personal services, the solicitor has the professional advantage. The client may feel that they cannot override the views of their legal adviser and may feel vulnerable in a relationship where the solicitor has the power.

In corporate practice, the client will have a lot of "buying power". The client determines the service standards they expect from the firm and they dictate the terms and conditions of business. The firm may have only a little flexibility in those terms in order to secure the lucrative work.

In-house lawyers are "owned" by the firm as much as any other employee is. It will be extremely difficult for the in-house lawyer to maintain independence from their employer. This can cause ethical dilemmas that need to be identified and monitored internally.

In-house legal departments need to ensure that they have robust systems and controls to ensure that these issues are regularly reviewed. Proper supervision is a key part of this system of checks and controls. Areas that can cause issues are where conflict of issues and confidentiality matters arise, particularly where the solicitor is providing advice to another client in the organisation or a work colleague whose interests may conflict with that of the employer.

The in-house lawyer needs to be adept at identifying the potential for issues to arise and to find the right solution to the unique challenges that they face.

Limitations of practice

In-house lawyers are limited in the way that they can practise. There is a specific publication produced by the SRA and Slaughter and May solicitors called *SRA Handbook 2011: In-house Lawyer Guide* to assist in-house lawyers to apply the Code of Conduct to their discrete area of work. In-house work is limited by the Legal Services Act 2007 and the Practice Framework Rules (PFR).

An in-house lawyer is not permitted to provide reserved legal services to the employer's clients, only to the employer. This is sometimes an area that can cause concern with large organisations. In-house lawyers can only advise their employer, a related body of their employer, a work colleague and members of the public on a pro bono basis, subject to restrictions.

For an in-house lawyer the first question they must consider is the identity of the client before they can ascertain their obligations to the client. This can be very simple if the employer is the only entity seeking advice from the solicitor. However, complications can arise when other individuals or entities within a large group seek advice. The ability to decipher the identity of the client is not likely to be an ethical issue. The PFR clearly set out the rules about who the client can be, so this is one hurdle that should be fairly easy to overcome. There is a fair amount of guidance in the PFR to help the in-house lawyer who they can advise.

If the solicitor decides that the client is someone who can be advised, the next issue is the type of duty that the solicitor owes to the client. In-house solicitors owe contractual and tortious duties to their client. The 10 Principles apply to in-house solicitors and the conflict and confidentiality chapters of the Code of Conduct are important.

4.5 Corporate lawyers

Not unlike the approach taken with in-house lawyers, corporate lawyers have a reputation for doing what it takes to satisfy their clients. The application of ethics may not come high on the list of personality traits to make a good corporate lawyer. This approach to over zealous lawyering with perhaps under zealous ethics application has come into the spotlight in a few cases over the last 5 years.

This may be changing with increasing numbers of corporate clients only hiring solicitors if ethics testing has taken place. This is particularly relevant with regards to diversity issues. The client holds the key to the importance of ethics in the corporate world it would seem. It is certainly true to say that the regulator doesn't seem to be regularly involved in controlling zealousness on the part of corporate lawyers.

The Law Society Gazette recently published an article in which they reported that MPs have criticised the SRA for failing to get involved in issues concerning a magic circle firm. There is a general view that the SRA takes a "light touch" approach when dealing with big firms.

Scenario: Disbursements

Facts

A city solicitor allowed taxi bills and secretarial overtime to be billed to clients as disbursements; this is usually taken to mean photocopying or scanning charges. No clients had complained about the solicitor's bills and they did not seek reimbursement from the firm.

Rules (the 2007 SCC applied in this case)

Principle 2: Act with integrity (these allegations were withdrawn by the SRA by agreement).

Principle 4: Failing to act in the best interests of his clients.

Principle 6: Behaving in a manner that was likely to diminish the trust placed in him and the legal profession.

Breaches

It is interesting to note that the solicitor was represented by Queen's Counsel at the preliminary hearings - the spending power of the solicitor is clearly contrasted against other ordinary solicitors, some of whom are not represented at all. All the remaining allegations were admitted by the solicitor who was fined £20,000 with a costs order of £38,000. The SDT said that it was unfortunate that the SRA had decided to deal with the case the way it had:

> *"This was particularly so where the impression may be given to the profession and to the public that the applicant was willing to discontinue serious allegations against a City lawyer when it was not often willing to do so against solicitors from smaller firms."*

Chapter 5: You v The Rest of the World

5.1 Introduction

What is the nature of the duty that solicitors owe to third parties? The SRA has dedicated Chapter 11 of the Code of Conduct to the nature of a solicitor's relations with others. The sometimes competing nature of the Principles and the Code mean that the solicitor can face any number of dilemmas on a daily basis.

In this chapter, we examine the solicitor's duties to others whilst acting for their client. Solicitors rarely act in isolation to third parties and so there are numerous people and organisations you can expect to deal with, including;

    (1)   The court

    (2)   Other solicitors

    (3)   The Land Registry

    (4)   Estate agents

    (5)   HMRC

    (6)   Companies House

    (7)   Litigants in Person

    (8)   McKenzie Friends

    (9)   Members of the Board if an ABS

    (10) Managers (non-lawyer)

    (11) Non-lawyer owners

    (12) Police

    (13) Social Services

    (14) Teachers

This list highlights the daily interactions a solicitor has with people and organisations other than their client. It is unlikely that a solicitor operates without any interaction with third parties.

Being a professional means that others should be able to interact with you reassured in the knowledge that your conduct is regulated to the highest standards. We previously explored the ethical behaviour of solicitors in Chapter 3 and so in this chapter we intend to highlight the fine balance of a solicitor's duties to third parties and the numerous ethical dimensions to be considered.

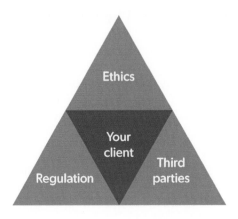

Fig 22: Your client is at the centre of decision-making but other issues surround your client and can't be ignored

5.2   The client above all else?

One of the principle ethical dilemmas faced by solicitors is the extent to which they owe a duty to their clients. As a solicitor, ask yourself these questions:

- Do you owe the client a duty to the **detriment** of everyone else?

- Do you **only** owe the client a duty to inform them about the law and then let them make ethical decisions going forward?

- Should the client be the first amongst equals with an **equal duty** to third parties after considering the client's position?

Solicitors in private practice may answer those questions very differently to solicitors who work in-house. In private practice, you will have exposure to numerous clients and the clients may change quickly within a year whereas if you work in-house, you have only one client. This means that the way you approach your client and the way they proceed when in possession of your advice will be very different. As we consider the regulatory and ethical issues the answers to these questions may change.

5.3   The Principles

Solicitors, by the very nature of their profession, have duties that extend beyond the client, even if that person is paying their fee. Whilst some would argue that the solicitor's main or only duty is to advance the interest of their client, the overarching SRA Principles counteract that view. This is sometimes difficult for the solicitor to grasp, given the complexities surrounding the nature of client relationships and the inevitable commercial pressures every solicitor faces.

The foundations

Fig 23: Two of the Principles operate against the world in general as opposed to the client individually

Naturally these are also combined with Principle 2 - solicitors **must** act with integrity. This matter is fully explored in Chapter 3. The combination of these Principles means that a solicitor needs to think carefully when interacting with third parties on behalf of a client.

Outcome (11.1): You do not take unfair advantage of third parties in either your professional or personal capacity

Having read the Chapter on "Virtue ethics - behaving ethically" you will be aware that it is expected that a solicitor will act with integrity at all times. Chapter 11 of the Code of Conduct specifies what type of behaviour is required by setting out the Outcomes and Indicative Behaviours expected from solicitors.

It is clear from the introduction to this chapter that the SRA focuses on the fact that solicitors should not take *unfair advantage* of third parties. After all, the professional capacity in which you act places you in a position that is thought of as being trustworthy to all and not just to your clients. The expected level of knowledge that the solicitor has puts them at a distinct advantage, which is why such knowledge should be used wisely.

There is no definition for the term "unfair advantage"; each case will turn on its own facts.

Scenario: Partnership agreement

Note that this isn't a regulatory case that was before the SRA or the Tribunal. This case was decided in the Court of Appeal.

Facts

Two solicitors had agreed to enter into partnership but didn't enter into a partnership agreement. Mr B thought he was owed money on his retirement and Ms H didn't agree. The Judge indicated that *"Mr B bears the greater responsibility for the failure of the parties to document their agreement and he may to a degree have taken advantage of Ms H's comparative lack of experience"*.

Plainly the fact that one had more experience than the other was a notable issue.

Solicitors are widely accepted as the face of the legal system and they have traditionally been situated on high streets across the country. Widely accessible to both paying and pro bono clients, they are at the coalface. Traditionally barristers have not been so easily accessible and although these roles are changing, the public perception of a solicitor and a barrister is likely to be different.

This client-facing role places a high ethical expectation on solicitors, more so than upon the ordinary non-professional employee. This is because solicitors are expected to show due care and skill and be seen to be upholding the rule of law generally. In fact, all qualified members of the legal profession carry similar ethical obligations, whether they are regulated by the SRA, the BSB or CILEx.

It is possible that the ethical expectations placed upon the shoulders of solicitors is higher than that expected from other types of professionals. If this is correct then the reason for the higher expectation could be that solicitors' skills have a higher impact/harm than perhaps the actions of an accountant. A recent survey holds lawyers in the top three of professionals trusted by the public; GPs came out on top with teachers coming second. Unsurprisingly, lawyers come out much better than politicians, bankers and journalists[6].

Every person whom a solicitor meets in the course of their life is entitled to hold them to account to exercise due care and skill, to adhere to the SRA Principles and to act within the ethical parameters set. This means that the solicitor must behave ethically at all times and not just between the hours of 9am and 5pm.

If, in your capacity as a solicitor, you send a document to a third party they are entitled to rely on the document. They should not question the veracity of the document - they are entitled to believe that you haven't tampered with the document in any way because you bear the title of "solicitor" and that means that you can be trusted. In recent years this has been tested by a number of banks who were sending letters to their clients that purported to be from separate solicitor's firms when in fact the letters were coming from the banks. It was reported in 2014 that in-house solicitors had been sending debt chasing letters to their clients, which purported to be in the name of firms that were in-house firms. When this practice was discovered it was felt that this could be a breach of Principle 6. In any event it didn't seem to be fully transparent behaviour.

An example of solicitors behaving in a way that is designed to help clients whilst balancing commercial realities is shown below.

Scenario: Criminal legal aid applications

Facts

It appears that there is a practice within some criminal practices to ask a client to sign a legal aid application form *before* the client has been charged with an offence. This practice has arisen recently as criminal solicitors now receive a fixed fee payment for attendance at a police station with the client. This means that they often won't be with the client at the point of charge - the form therefore needs to be signed by the client in advance.

Arguably the action is carried out for the right reason - it is in the client's best interests as it ensures that they are represented at the first hearing.

---

[6] *In Professions We Trust - Fostering virtuous practitioners in teaching, law and medicine*

Potential ethical/professional breaches

By dating the form on a date after charge, which will be different to the date that the client signed the form, the solicitor is representing to the Legal Aid Agency that the form was signed by the client on that day, which is clearly not the case.

The conveyancing solicitor will hold a signed transfer deed to be dated on the day of transfer. Does this differ from the criminal solicitor holding a signed legal aid form waiting for the client to be charged?

The solicitor's duty to the third party is to ensure that the proper administration of justice is done. The solicitor's duty to the client is to ensure that they are able to represent the client at the court hearing and that legal aid is arranged for that purpose.

Suggested action

Arguably, the client's interests could be met by asking the client to attend the office to sign the forms after charge and before the hearing. There are practical issues with this course of action as it can be difficult to get clients to take an interest in the paperwork. The duty to the client is equal to that of the duty to the third party.

In the alternative, the solicitor could re-attend the client at the point of charge, but of course there are fee implications of doing this.

Compare this to the conveyancer who holds the signed transfer deed or contract; all parties in that transaction know that the documents have been signed pending exchange of contracts and completion. Does the Legal Aid Agency know that the forms are being signed in advance and kept on the file? If so, does the LAA regulate against such action?

There are both ethical and regulatory considerations when taking on board Principle 6 in the above scenario; it is possible that the duty to the third party is greater than the standalone duty to the client.

There are many of you who could not conceive of such actions happening regularly, but we imagine there are at least an equal number who would not see this as an ethical or regulatory matter.

There are numerous examples from the SDT judgments of solicitors who have "tampered" with documents.

Scenario: Declaration of Trust

Facts

Solicitor N created a Declaration of Trust, which he submitted to the Land Registry. The document purported to be created in 2004 when in fact it had been created in 2007. In addition, he submitted to his lender clients incorrect or incomplete information about transaction values for a series of related transactions for the same clients. There were allegations of dishonesty levied against Solicitor N.

Regulatory matters

The solicitor admitted all breaches of the Rules and Regulations, which were brought under the Solicitors' Code of Conduct 2007. He denied the allegation of dishonesty.

In creating the Deed of Declaration of Trust and sending it to the Land Registry as though it had been created on the earlier date Solicitor N plainly intended to mislead. Solicitor N explained his reasoning to the investigating officer as follows:

> *"Well, as I said, I perceived the whole titling circumstances to be a mess, they needed to be tidied up, quickly and at a minimum of cost and that wrongly was to save stamp duty and in fact didn't, I mean, what's crazy about it is that it didn't have to, we didn't have to put that in to do that because there was a common shareholding, it was exempt stamp duty, but it was wrong and I put my hands up."*

Outcome

In respect of this allegation the Tribunal found that the motivation was financial gain for the client. The conduct was not capable of being anything but dishonest. For this and the 4 other breaches and a further finding of dishonesty Solicitor N was struck off. He was ordered to pay costs of £22,424.55.

Steps to avoid

Solicitor N made no additional money over his firm's fees as a result of his involvement in these property transactions. His actions were undertaken purely to assist his clients. He said when interviewed that he probably backdated the Deed of Declaration to save his clients stamp duty. He did not need to take this step, as the transaction was stamp duty exempt.

The solicitor shouldn't have been so accommodating to a big property developer generating fairly substantial fees for the firm.

On the facts of this case, the solicitor was as accommodating as possible, probably to keep the client happy to keep the work. He seemed not to realise at the time he did it that he had stepped over the line between ethical and unethical.

5.4   Undertakings

Regulatory matters

An undertaking is a binding promise to do something, which allows the smooth running of legal processes. An undertaking is usually given to other solicitors or legal professionals or to the court. Undertakings have a high status of reliance placed upon them and are equally valid whether stated orally or in writing. Much of the work of conveyancers would be unfeasible if not for undertakings given to banks and the other side's solicitors.

Outcome (11.2) states that a solicitor must:

> *"perform all undertakings given by you within an agreed timescale or within a reasonable amount of time".*

Because undertakings can be given and accepted orally, there is wide scope for misinterpretation as to the exact terms of the undertaking. This can extend to situations when parties wonder whether a conversation resulted in an undertaking being given at all. It should be clear whether an undertaking is being offered and if so, that the undertaking is made clearly. It is also important to check that the person giving the undertaking has sufficient authority to do so.

Solicitors will only give undertakings that they can fulfil as they remain personally liable; however the undertaking also binds the firm. It is both unethical and impractical to give undertakings knowing that they are not capable of being fulfilled. This would not be viewed as a solicitor upholding the proper administration of justice.

A request for an undertaking to ensure that your client will do something or perform an act shouldn't be given by a solicitor as they aren't able to ensure that the client can fulfil the undertaking. If the solicitor is minded to give the undertaking it should be carefully worded.

Fig 24: How undertakings work

A solicitor should only ever give an undertaking that is possible to perform personally, or on behalf of the firm if authorised to do so - for example to send documents to the court or the other side within a specified timescale.

The solicitor enjoys a privileged position as to the reliance third parties can place on their undertakings. The undertaking of a solicitor is their bond and the giving of an undertaking is an important and actionable matter. Bear in mind that when giving a third party an undertaking the solicitor must be seen to be administering the proper application of the legal system. The solicitor also needs to bear in the mind the potential for third party damages.

When things go wrong

Prima facie, a breach of an undertaking given by a solicitor is interpreted as professional misconduct and there is usually only one exception to this rule. This is if the undertaking is given to the court as only the court has the power to enforce sanctions for the breach. Usually no other action would be taken save for the action of the court. See for example, CCR Order 29 Rule 2(1) which states that; "*An undertaking given by a solicitor in relation to any proceeding in a county court may be enforced, by order of the judge of that court, by committal order against the solicitor*".

Although another party to the proceedings can apply to have the order enforced by committal an application needs to be submitted with an affidavit attached.

Where the undertaking is given to the court the proper sanction should be imposed by the court and not by the regulator. Naturally the breach of an undertaking is also taken as a serious reputational matter. As there is no obligation on a firm to give or accept undertakings it is perfectly possible that a firm that doesn't fulfil an undertaking will find in the future that their undertakings are refused.

The court, the SRA, Law Society and SDT will take a dim view of a solicitor breaching an undertaking. Even where circumstances have changed from the time that the undertaking was given, the giver of the undertaking would be expected to fulfil the promise. Enforcing an undertaking is seen as upholding the proper administration of the legal system.

Scenario: Undertaking

Facts

In a family law matter, solicitors undertook not to release the passport to their client, the father in the proceedings. On the strength of that undertaking he was granted an order to see his children.

Rules

Principle 1: Uphold the rule of law and the proper administration of justice.

Principle 6: Act in a way which maintains the trust the public places in the profession.

Outcome (11.2): Perform all undertakings given by you within an agreed timescale or within a reasonable amount of time.

Breach

The solicitors wrongly released their client's passport to him in breach of their undertaking. Father absconded out of the country, with the children.

Outcome

The wife successfully sued the firm in negligence - they owed her and the children a duty of care when they gave the undertaking.

5.5 Undertakings - Policies, systems and controls

In the above example, the failure to comply with the undertaking was an administrative error which caused great upheaval to the parties and the children. Due to the serious nature of undertakings and the potential regulatory and reputational damage that may be caused by failing to fulfil them, firms should devise systems and policies to control risk. These systems and policies are designed to both record any undertakings and also the time and method applied to discharge those undertakings.

Whilst this might seem purely a regulatory matter, the interpretation of an undertaking can include ethical considerations. For example, if a solicitor gave the following undertaking: *"we undertake not to release our client's passport to him"*, there are a number of possible interpretations.

This is where the ethical solicitor will interpret the undertaking to their highest obligation, meaning: *"we should never release this passport to this client"*.

An ethically minimalist solicitor might release the client's passport to him in the event that he no longer retains the services of the firm. After all, the undertaking says "our client's passport". Therefore, if he is no longer a client, then the firm can't be held responsible. It is splitting hairs to make that distinction but there are solicitors who would do this if their client wanted his passport to be returned to him. In the above example, there was a simple administrative error that should have been avoided when looking at the outcome for the children.

Systems and policies are also designed to comply with Indicative Behaviours IB(11.5) and IB(11.6). The firm should be able to demonstrate to the SRA that they have assessed the risk and made provision to mitigate the potential risks. However, these systems are also important to ensure that solicitors behave ethically and not just in a regulatory manner. It would be wrong to believe that the giving of an undertaking is merely just an administrative matter. Where there are any issues about the wording of the undertaking, it should be interpreted in the strictest manner possible, from the perspective of "the ethical solicitor". Solicitors who give undertakings should be certain about what they mean in letter and in spirit and ensure that the wording of the undertaking is as specific as it should be.

When giving an undertaking you may wish to make provision for what would happen if the person who gave the undertaking isn't around when the act needs to be completed (e.g. due to resignation or illness). A suitably robust recording system should be developed so the firm knows exactly what undertakings were taken, what tasks the firm or solicitor must undertake and when they have to be completed in order to reduce their risk.

Firms need policies and procedures to ensure that undertakings are properly recorded but this does not replace the need for good training with regard to proper conduct relating to undertakings. The placement of a good policy does not act as a "get out of jail free" card with regard to third parties. Like many things, the policy aspects are there to ensure compliance to the spirit of the rule and not just the letter.

5.6 Do solicitors have an obligation to correct mistakes of third parties?

Most solicitors would view their primary responsibility to be to serve the best interests of their client as discussed above. The firm will want to make profits and maintain a commercial view about the "business of law". These two tensions and the impact they have on ethical behaviour are examined in more detail in other chapters.

Consider this by Lord Phillips of Sudbury:

"In a country awash with evermore law and regulation of baffling complexity, lawyers are commensurately indispensable as the gatekeepers of justice. Yet the truth is that we are increasingly obsessed with our own profit. The idea of lawyering being a vocation, or a profession, seems out of date to many solicitors who consider themselves just business people."

It is therefore important to keep in mind that solicitors hold a special place in society. To regard the legal professional merely as a collection of businesses with the disadvantage of compliance and ethical handcuffs is entirely at odds with the ethos and behaviours expected of them.

What happens if the other side has made an error of law and the litigation or transaction is likely to be resolved based on an error? We consider the ethical considerations on the solicitor in these circumstances. The manner in which a solicitor behaves might be different if the other side is unrepresented or not.

The main Principles that the solicitor has to consider are indicated below:

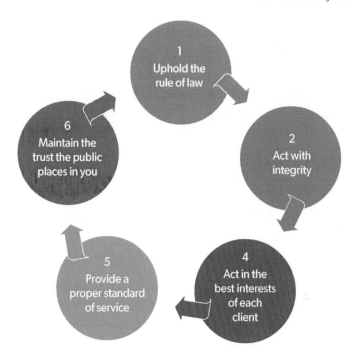

Fig 25: The 5 main Principles a solicitor needs to consider

In addition to the above mandatory principles, the Code of Conduct at IB(11.7) states that we should not take unfair advantage of an opposing party's lack of legal knowledge where they have not instructed a lawyer.

Scenario: Conveyancing

Facts

The buyers' solicitor discovers a defective deed which the sellers signed when they purchased the property. It requires the sellers to pay an additional annual service charge for the maintenance of land near the property. The sellers' solicitor doesn't ask the buyers to take over responsibility for the payment by entering into a deed.

Should the buyers' solicitor highlight the issue to the sellers' solicitor? If so, this will result in an annual charge to the buyers.

Rules

As per diagram above.

Potential ethical issues/professional breaches

If the buyers' solicitor highlights the matter to them together with the obligation to uphold the proper administration of justice, the clients might not be too happy to proceed forward.

If the solicitor doesn't notify the sellers' solicitor about the matter then the sellers will remain responsible for the charges which will relate to a property that they have sold. They are not likely to believe that the buyers' solicitor has acted with integrity if they find out that he knew about the defect. It is highly unlikely they would ever discover this fact.

There could be negligence issues that they will take up with their solicitors.

Possible approaches

- The buyers' solicitor can raise the issue with the buyers and let them decide how they want to proceed.
- The buyers' solicitor raises the matter with the other side without asking the buyers (Principles 1, 2 and 6 over Principle 4). [Is this the path of the ethical solicitor?]
- The buyers' solicitor doesn't mention the matter to either the buyers or to the sellers' solicitor (Principle 4 takes priority). [Ethically minimalist?]

Suggested reaction/steps to avoid

Communicating the issue to the clients means that the clients are able to make a fully informed decision about the way forward.

If they decide that they don't want the matter raised then this is a decision for them.

However, the solicitor may take the view that they should bring the matter to the attention to the sellers' solicitor as there may be an action in negligence against the original solicitors who didn't notice that the deed was defective.

5.7 Mistakes where the other side is represented by a solicitor

Most solicitors would say that it is up to the opposing solicitor to be both up to date with the law and have the proper skill set to both interpret and apply the law to a professional standard. After all, Principle 5 makes this clear - you need to provide a proper level of service to your clients. From 1 November 2016, this, in combination with the Statement of Legal Knowledge, means that you need to demonstrate an appropriate level of competence to practise law.

Each solicitor is required to ensure that he or she can demonstrate competence against a Statement of Competence written by the SRA. Each solicitor needs to assess if they meet the correct standard against the "threshold criteria", also published by the SRA.

If the opposing solicitor makes a mistake, their client can sue them in negligence. Many of you will think that is just bad luck - it is up to each solicitor to get the best result for their client. If you make a mistake which is picked up, you have a positive duty to disclose it to your client.

Failing to draw attention to the other side's mistake could lead to an awful lot of stress and expense for the other solicitor's client who may need to apply to rectify the mistake or seek redress. Is it ethical for the solicitor to "keep quiet"? Or is it more important to keep your client happy? Is it possible to keep everyone happy (including the regulator)?

Your response to this particular kind of problem will rest on the specific error:

- Is it a simple "typo" style of mistake? Has the other side put 56% instead of 65%?

- Is there a misunderstanding about the law? The other side thinks A when actually B is the case.

- Has the other side overlooked something? In the conveyancing example above the other side has overlooked the existence of the poorly drafted deed and continuing liability of the sellers to pay the service charge.

In all of these cases, it is a difficult balancing act between championing your client's interests and the other Principles - ultimately the decision will be an ethical one. The ethical solicitor will always act in a completely transparent way to ensure that all mistakes and misunderstandings are cleared up before an agreement is entered into.

Regulatory Principles clash

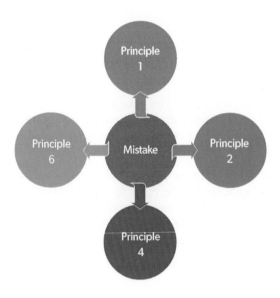

Fig 26: When regulatory Principles clash

5.8   Mistakes where the other side is a litigant in person

The Principles and the Code of Conduct are clear in this area - it is difficult for solicitors to proceed on the basis of a mistake, particularly where the other side is not represented. IB(11.7) states that if you act in a way that takes advantage of the other side where they have not instructed a lawyer then it will tend to show that you haven't achieved the regulatory outcomes. The Law Society have a practice note on dealing with Litigants in Person (LiPs) which should be consulted as it provides excellent practical guidance.

When is a LiP a LiP?

It is, however, sometimes difficult to ascertain if LiPs are actually unrepresented as LiPs can be:

- completely without legal advice because they can't afford it;
- completely without legal advice because they don't want it;
- advised by a legal adviser who isn't on the record as acting;
- advised at court but not in the conduct of litigation generally.

Ask yourself these questions:

    (1)   What category does the other side fall into?

    (2)   How does that impact on your responsibility to deal with mistakes?

    (3)   What are your regulatory and ethical considerations?

There are shades of grey in the above categories and your ethical compass will need to be fully engaged in these situations.

Scenario: Litigant in Person

Facts

The LiP husband is represented in Family Court proceedings by a direct access barrister. There are no solicitors on record for the LiP.

The barrister makes a mistake when drafting an order which means that his client (the applicant) will be responsible for the payment of costs of implementation of certain parts of the order. [We do not propose to consider the barrister's regulatory, conduct and ethical issues within the confines of this book.]

Rules

Principles: *1, 2, 4,* and *6* as above

Ethical considerations

You are a solicitor acting for the respondent and you decide not to say anything to highlight the barrister's mistake, which comes from the barrister's lack of knowledge rather than an administrative error. You take the view that you aren't taking advantage of a third party as the barrister is a professional who doesn't bring up the issue of costs. The default position will leave his client bearing the administrative costs of implementation.

When dealing with the implementation of the order you are once again dealing with the LiP who doesn't engage the services of a solicitor when out of court. You ask him for the costs of the implementation of the order (£1,000 plus VAT) so that the order can be implemented in your client's favour. The LiP won't pay as he says that he didn't know anything about the costs. You make him aware that he may have a claim against his barrister but that the deal is done and he needs to pay up.

Outcome

This isn't necessarily a fantastic result for the public perception of the law and solicitors in general. You may have done the best thing for your client in the short term, saving them fees of £1,000.

Have you taken "unfair" advantage of the barrister who should have known about the charge? Although the barrister is qualified it is possible (in the view of the SRA) for a solicitor to take advantage of a barrister. It isn't wholly transparent that you didn't raise the issue of the costs at the hearing. The other side's redress may be against the barrister rather than you as the solicitor. The regulatory position is slightly murky on this point.

The question is whether the actions of the solicitor are **ethical** or not. In the long term your client may not prosper as this is likely to cause the need for the matter to return to court for enforcement proceedings if the applicant refuses to pay the costs. Implementation of the order will be delayed as the costs aren't paid. Keeping quiet to secure an advantage isn't transparent and so might not be viewed as entirely ethical.

Arguably, Principles 5 and 6 have not been met; there will be a further delay to the conclusion of matters for your client. The LiP will certainly feel let down by the legal system but whether this is rectified by pursuing the barrister or not is outside the scope of this book.

Solicitors are dealing with increasing numbers of LiPs in practice and you need to be aware of the duty owed to them from a regulatory standpoint. Ethically, it is obvious that the need to be fully open and transparent with the LiP is absolute as in the following example[7].

Scenario: Abuse of process

Facts

In 2015 a father (H) made an application to the High Court seeking to put his ex-partner's solicitor in prison for the way that she acted during Children Act proceedings. He also made applications against other professionals who were joined to the action.

---

[7] *H v Dent & Ors [2015] EWHC 2090 (Fam)*

The defendants made an application to strike out the committal application as an abuse of process.

Father alleged that the solicitor deceived him and the lay justices about the state of the law when they were at a final hearing. He alleged that as the solicitor is a specialist in international law, "her deception and contempt" was not an accidental matter.

He also complained that the matter should have been dealt with at a higher judicial level and that the solicitor should have brought this to the attention of the law justices.

In support of his application, he produced a number of audio tapes of illicit recordings he had taken at the court.

Regulations

As above - *Principles 1, 2, 4*, and *6* and *Outcome (11.7)*

Outcome

The court stated that the complaints against the solicitor "completely ignores the fact that her professional duties lay with her own client".

The judge in that matter went on to say: "She had no contractual relationship with H and at no time was her professional relationship with him impressed with any fiduciary or legal obligations".

The court acknowledged that the solicitor had a duty not to mislead the court and that there was no evidence that she had done so. There was no evidence that he didn't give his true consent to the terms of the order at the final hearing.

H's applications for committal were struck out as there were no disclosable grounds for bringing the application and it was an abuse of process to do so. The applicant had failed to observe procedural matters and the judge would not allow him to rectify those matters.

Ethical matters

If the father in this case made a complaint to the SRA it may be that the result would be the same. After all, the criminal standard of proof must be met in both. However, it may be that the information the solicitor gave the father fell short of the transparent ethical manner in which she should have dealt with a LiP (although there is nothing to suggest in reading this judgment that this was the case).

The point is that the public at large feel that solicitors owe them a "duty of care" even if they aren't paying for their services. They feel that they should be able to trust the information (falling short of advice) given to them by a solicitor.

5.9   The proper administration of oaths, affirmations or declarations

In the administration of oaths, affirmations and declarations, the solicitor owes a duty to more people and organisations than just their own client.

Although the regulations don't specify the rules about making changes to other documents, it is largely accepted that documents shouldn't be changed after signature.

Scenario: Forging signatures

Facts

A solicitor's clerk was accused of forging various solicitors' signatures on a number of documents - one was a certified copy of a document, and another was a statutory declaration.

Although in this case there was found to be no case to answer due to the quality of the evidence, it highlights that a solicitor's signature on a document is an important matter.

Rules

The SRA wished to prove that the fee earner was guilty of breaches of Principles 1, 2 and 6. Although his guilt wasn't established, it is important to note that the issues were treated on a par despite the fact that the regulations specifically mention the administration of oaths and not signing other documents.

Outcomes

The matter was dismissed against the clerk, albeit he had initially accepted his wrongdoing in respect of one matter during an internal disciplinary meeting.

Ethical considerations

Solicitors should know that altering a document after signature without consent of the client is not ethical behaviour.

5.10 Fees paid by third parties

Litigation solicitors will know that often their client's fees can now be paid for by third parties. It is quite common for groups with stakes in the outcome of a case to provide funds, where the litigant themselves may have difficulty doing so. Insurance companies, trade unions, charities and various pressure groups may pay the litigation fees for particular cases as they have an interest in the outcome.

Scenario: Third party funding

Facts

In a recent family litigation case, the fees of the wife were paid for by investors for the first time. After the case was disposed of by the High Court, with an award of £20 million to the wife, the investors are allegedly about to sue her for breach for contract. The investors allege that the wife used some of the money they gave her for purposes other than to fund her legal fees. She denies the allegations.

In these situations, it is important that the solicitor remembers that the duty is to the client, not to the party who is actually paying the fees. As the matter progresses the interests of the litigant and the third party may diverge, as can be seen in the example above.

Third party litigation funding is more common in commercial cases and research indicates that its use has shot up over the last six years. The Justice NOT Profit campaign says that the industry has outgrown self-regulation. In 2009, Lord Justice Jackson said that if the use of this type of funding increased to a point of significance then the full statutory regulation would be required. Falling short of that, ethical considerations become ever more important. 63% of those polled said they were either quite or very concerned about the increase in for-profit third party funding.

Fees paid by third parties give rise to many compliance and ethical issues:

- Confidentiality (SRA Code of Conduct Chapter 4);
- Acting in the best interests of your client (Principle 4);
- Behaving in a way that maintains the trust the public places in you and the provision of legal services (Principle 6).

The ethical issues arise when there is likely to be a conflict between what is in the best interests of the client and what is best for the entity funding the case.

It is advisable for the solicitor in this situation to be clear with the client and third party how the solicitor will deal with the case. This is likely to come in the form of agreements drawn up by the funder as to how the litigation should be conducted. After all, a "for-profit" funder will want to ensure that there will be success at the end of the day otherwise there will be no profit to share. At the start of the case the interests of the client and the funder are aligned; both want to achieve financial redress at the end of the case. There are a few issues that the solicitor will need to think about at that stage .

However, as the matter moves forward, the way in which the litigation progresses may illicit different responses from the funder and the client. The client may have emotional reasons for wanting to proceed to a trial and cross-examination. The client may have unrealistic ideas of success and may not recognise a good offer of settlement when they see one. On the other hand, a professional third party litigation funder will have very fixed ideas about the progress of litigation and settlement options. There will be no emotion attached to the decision; the decisions will centre on profit for the funder. This is where the solicitor may feel a conflict between the two parties.

From a regulatory perspective, it is important to record the boundaries that exist between the client and the funder. More often than not, the funder will have strict terms under which it is willing to proceed. These duties will be documented, and the solicitor must ensure that the client is aware of them and that they are willing and able to fulfil those obligations.

It can be difficult to tread the ethical line between the client and the funder regarding the case, its merits and the evidence. Solicitors can very easily find themselves in a difficult position where their obligations to the funder and the client conflict.

5.11 Multiple clients

The arrangements between the solicitor and both parties must be sufficient for the size and complexity of the matter. For instance if the matter is a complex class action the solicitor needs to have a clear and effective governance structure with clear reporting lines setting out what information can be shared about any one individual matter. Never has there been a greater need to ensure that each client's interests are protected.

When drawing up any such arrangements, the solicitor would need to pay particular attention to:

- *Outcome (1.2)*: you provide services to your clients in a manner which protects their interests in their matter, subject to the proper administration of justice;

- *Outcome (1.6)*: you only enter into fee agreements with your clients that are legal, and which you consider are suitable for the client's needs and take account of the client's best interests;

- *Outcome (9.1)*: your independence and your professional judgement are not prejudiced by virtue of any arrangement with another person;

- *Outcome (1.14)*: clients are informed of their right to challenge or complain about your bill and the circumstances in which they may be liable to pay interest on an unpaid bill;

- *Outcome (1.15)*: you properly account to clients for any financial benefit you receive as a result of your instructions.

5.12 Contacting the opposing party or their McKenzie Friend

As a rule a solicitor should not contact the other party directly if they have legal representation. This is one rule that should only be flexible in extreme circumstances. The Code of Conduct is quite explicit about this as it states:

"You do not communicate with another party when you are aware that the other party has retained a lawyer in a matter, except:

(a) to request the name and address of the other party's lawyer; or

(b) the other party's lawyer consents to you communicating with the client; or

(c) where there are exceptional circumstances."

Where the other party has not yet instructed a solicitor then of course it is necessary to communicate with them. The Law Society practice note on dealing with Litigants in Person[8] is very helpful in circumstances where contact with the other side is unavoidable. A solicitor can be accused of being in breach of O(11.1) by acting in a way set out in IB(11.7) - taking unfair advantage of an opposing party's lack of legal knowledge where they have not instructed a lawyer. This is discussed above and needs to be borne in mind. It is also possible that the LiP isn't clear about the role of the solicitor in proceedings and can view them with hostility, making it very difficult for the client to observe his or her regulatory functions.

In the case where the opposing party has engaged the services of an unqualified person, then ethical issues arise alongside regulatory concerns. In the current legal market place, there are unregulated paralegal firms and McKenzie Friend services who compete against solicitors for work. Where this is the case, the qualified solicitor needs to tread carefully in his or her communication with unqualified and unregulated entities.

---

[8] *Produced by The Law Society in conjunction with CILEx and the Bar Council. Available on The Law Society website, June 2015*

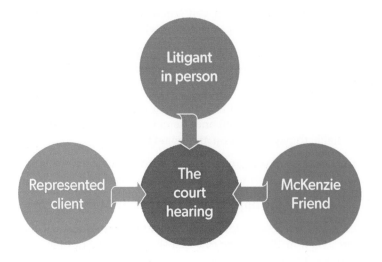

Fig 27: Parties attending a court hearing

All parties are permitted to attend hearings (McKenzie Friends only with permission); however the court should not accept any communication with the McKenzie Friend that would be covered under the banner "reserved legal activities". Unless the McKenzie Friend is given permission by the court they are not permitted to provide advocacy services or conduct litigation. If they do this they will commit a criminal offence. This extends to paralegal firms as they are not authorised entities.

This means that the solicitor should not entertain correspondence with the unregulated firm as this could be a breach of duty to their own client. Bear in mind that the unregulated entity may have no data protection in place; they have no regulated Code of Conduct and may even distribute your client's information deliberately if instructed to do so by their client. Often these firms are not only unregulated but also uninsured. Whilst their "client" will want you to communicate with them, your duty is to your client in this situation and not the third party.

Any dealings with an unqualified person fall under O(11.1): "you do not take unfair advantage of third parties in either your professional or personal capacity". Any communications you have with an unregulated third party should be civil.

It some circumstances it might be helpful to be able to communicate with the McKenzie Friend who might be able to bring about a settlement or narrow issues. However, only the LiP has the right to conduct the litigation and no other person. They're not in a position to authorise another person in their place, even by way of a power of attorney. The problem then can be the fact that the best thing for your client will be to communicate with the third party but by doing so you would be encouraging them to break the law by conducting litigation. If you find that you are in this position, the court has the power to authorise the McKenzie Friend to conduct litigation. This is much rarer than a McKenzie Friend being permitted to advocate on behalf of a client in court. The Law Society practice note indicates that:

> *"You should not communicate directly with an MF, but address all communications to the LiP. If a LiP uses an MF, the MF cannot appear in court unless the LiP is also present."*

5.13 Stealing clients

Is it ethical for a solicitor to take another solicitor's client?

This is an ethical conundrum that comes up in all practice areas, some more so than others. To put the issue in sharper focus we will use the example below.

Scenario: Stealing clients

Facts

Solicitor A takes on a client to do some work which isn't in his specialist area. He is hoping to expand his work base and as he is a sole practitioner it would suit him (and his profit margins) to develop a new work stream. The client has received his client care letter and his terms and conditions of business. She has agreed an hourly rate that is more than the published solicitor's guidance hourly rates for a solicitor of his experience.

As part of his job to find suitable funding for the client to pursue her case, she needs to get some advice about the funding agreement from an independent solicitor so she makes an appointment to see Solicitor B. Solicitor B is a specialist in this field of work with more than 12 years' experience.

Both Solicitor A and B are sole practitioners; Solicitor A undertakes a variety of work and Solicitor B only takes on work in his specialist field.

Solicitor A receives an email from Solicitor B asking for the file of papers to be transferred to him as the client has decided to move firms. He attaches an authority from the client requesting the transfer.

The client suffers from depression and is seeing a counsellor. The client refuses to communicate with Solicitor A following the appointment with Solicitor B.

Regulations

Principle 2: Act with integrity.

Principle 6: Behave in a way that maintains the trust the public places in you and in the provision of legal services.

Outcome (1.1): Treat your clients fairly.

Outcome (1.4): Have the resources, skills and procedures to carry out your client's instructions.

Outcome (1.5): The service you provide to your clients is competent, delivered in a timely manner and takes account of your clients' needs and circumstances.

Outcome (1.16): Inform current client if you discover any act or omission which could give rise to a claim by them against you.

Outcome (11.1): Do not take unfair advantage of third parties in either your professional or personal capacity.

Potential ethical/regulatory breaches

Solicitor A

He has taken on work in a field that he is not an expert in. However, he does meet the required standard of competence as set out by the SRA for a day 1 qualified solicitor in the new area of work. He has undertaken a number of courses in the new field and he isn't holding himself out as a specialist. He should therefore meet O(1.4) and O(1.5). It is not unusual for solicitors to practise in more than one area of law.

He has not done anything that would result in a claim being made against him.

He might be billing the client more than an experienced solicitor would but the client has had all the billing information that the solicitor is required to send.

There are no apparent regulatory breaches by Solicitor A.

Are there any ethical breaches as Solicitor A isn't a specialist in the field and is charging more than the guideline rates for his year of qualification and location? This isn't a regulatory breach but when taking on board a new area of work should the solicitor be charging lower fees while he finds his feet so that the client doesn't suffer from his lack of experience? Would the public believe that his actions are not trustworthy for a solicitor?

Solicitor B

Solicitor B was engaged to give advice about a funding arrangement and not the case as a whole. It is not known what Solicitor B said to the client to persuade her to change solicitors. It would however appear that he overstepped the boundaries of his retainer - this is not in itself a regulatory breach.

Taking into account the fact that the client is vulnerable, did Solicitor B take these steps to protect the client or has Solicitor B taken advantage of her vulnerable position? At the time that Solicitor B spoke to the client, he owed her a duty as she was his client as well as Solicitor A's client. He was under an obligation to treat her fairly. Solicitor B may have believed that his own experience as a specialist solicitor was greater than that being offered by Solicitor A and that the client should be made aware of that matter.

He also owed Solicitor A a duty to ensure that he treated him professionally and he was under an obligation not to take unfair advantage of him as a third party. It is not known if Solicitor B used his greater experience to persuade the client to change firms.

Neither is it known if Solicitor B was acting with integrity in his communications with the client about Solicitor A. It is questionable whether this type of client poaching is considered acceptable by the public or if this would be considered to be a breach of trust issue.

It would appear from the facts of the case that there is no regulatory issue in taking a client from another firm in the way that Solicitor B has done. Depending on the specific circumstances of the case and what was said to the client by Solicitor B, he may have believed that he was acting in the client's best interests if Solicitor A was charging over the guideline hourly rates.

Solicitor B's charging rates were slightly higher than Solicitor A's but also in excess of the hourly rates guidelines. Could the higher charging rate easily be justified as he had many years of specialist experience? Is it ever ethically acceptable to charge more than the guideline rates and should both solicitors have informed the client that they are charging more than recommended?

Suggested reaction

Both solicitors should revisit their hourly charging rate to see if they are happy charging more than the guideline hourly rates. If they decide to charge these rates going forward should they highlight to prospective clients why they believe they should charge more?

Solicitor A should not send his clients to firms that he doesn't have a business relationship with. He should ensure in future that the firms he refers these clients to are not going to take his clients. Whilst the behaviour isn't likely to be a breach of regulations, it may be viewed in many sectors as unethical behaviour.

In a more commercial setting this issue is unlikely to cause much consternation as commercial clients are savvy enough to make sensible buying decisions about legal services. They are aware of their choices, buying power, experience of solicitors and guideline hourly rates.

In a more personal legal situation the client might not be a sophisticated purchaser of legal services or they may be vulnerable and an approach to change solicitor must be viewed in the proper context.

Solicitor B should be careful about populating his clients from other firms as this may damage his reputation and that of his firm in the future. It is likely that once reputational damage is done to the firm that other solicitors will not refer clients to the firm if it is believed that the solicitor has acted unethically.

5.14 Demanding anything for yourself or the client that is not legally recoverable

In the SRA's Code of Conduct relating to your dealings with third parties they suggest that there are indicative behaviours that indicate whether or not you are not meeting the stated outcome. That outcome is set out at length above.

IB(11.8) states that if you are "demanding anything for yourself or on behalf of your client, that is not legally recoverable, such as when you are instructed to collect a simple debt, demanding from the debtor the cost of the letter of claim since it cannot be said at that stage that such a cost is legally recoverable" then you aren't demonstrating compliance with O(11.1).

Firstly, it is likely to be accepted by most solicitors that demanding something from a third party for yourself is not likely to be ethical or compliant with the regulations.

However, the second limb throws up ethical issues and a conflict between the duty to your client and that to a third party. It is worthwhile recalling the issue of the in-house solicitors writing letters that looked as though they came from separate firms. Litigators can be prone to sending letters with the veiled (or clear) threat of legal costs in the event that a certain course of action is or isn't followed. This can add urgency to proceedings and can encourage parties to think more carefully about the next steps.

Scenario: Recoverable costs

Facts

A solicitor acting for a judgment creditor writes to the judgment debtor setting out the case. If the debt isn't paid with interest within 7 days then enforcement proceedings will be sought and a costs order will be pursued. The debt isn't paid and the solicitor writes once more stating that an application has been sent for a charging order and that the judgment creditor will seek a costs order, the costs incurred so far being £1,000 plus VAT and court fees.

Regulations

The issue with the above scenario is the fact that the only costs that can be recovered in this type of action are fixed costs. The fact that the costs are £1,000 plus VAT will have no bearing on that fact that the costs are fixed at £110 plus reasonable disbursements. Is the solicitor doing the best for the client? Or is the solicitor taking advantage of an unrepresented third party?

Ethical considerations

Is it ethical to lead a third party to believe that they could be liable for costs of £1,000 plus VAT or should the solicitor be explicit that the costs will be capped at £110? The letter itself doesn't say that the costs order will be made in the sum of £1,000 plus VAT. It doesn't even say that the costs order requested will be for the sum of £1,000 plus VAT but it certainly gives the impression that the costs that could be ordered will be £1,000 plus VAT.

Is it ethical to allow a LiP believe something that isn't be true?

5.15 Taking unfair advantage of another person in order to advance your personal interests

IB(11.9) says that using your professional status or qualification to take unfair advantage of another person in order to advance your personal interests could be in breach of O(11.1). Have you ever sent a personal letter and added "solicitor" or "LLB Hons" at the foot of your signature to make an impression? Were you hoping that your letter of complaint to John Lewis would be taken more seriously if they see your qualifications?

If so you may have behaved in a way that the SRA would see as being in breach of O(11.1). You intended to use your position of professional influence to work in your favour against a third party. This would include any comments along the line of "I'm a solicitor, I know the law" when returning (faulty) goods and hoping for a refund rather than store credit.

This should give all solicitors pause for thought.

5.16 Conclusion

Although solicitors would like to ensure that his or her client has the best possible opportunity of securing the best result, this must be done within regulatory and ethical guidelines.

It can be seen from the example above that a solicitor suggesting a proposed course of settlement of a case can be easily misconstrued by a LiP as securing an unfair advantage. There is a fine line to be walked and solicitors must be careful to ensure that they are mindful of zealously representing their own client's interests and infringing those of third parties.

The ethical solicitor should therefore have in the front of his or her mind the fact that being a professional brings with it serious obligations to the world at large. The ethical solicitor will always err on the side of caution in his or her dealings with third parties, especially where those parties are LiPs. The SRA has also indicated that it is possible for a solicitor to take unfair advantage of counsel as a third party and this is an additional burden to bear. One can't assume equality of arms against another legal professional if they are younger, less experienced or just not very good at their job - it is possible that the SRA will see this as a solicitor's breach.

The ethically minimalist solicitor will often make decisions which are not the same as their more ethical peers. They will not err on the side of caution. Instead, they hope that they stay on the right side of regulations and compliance without really assessing whether this will be the case.

The way you choose to practise will change and develop over time but the way the world sees you is just as important as the way your client sees you. The only difference is that your client is probably the one paying your bill.

Chapter 6: Complaints and negligence

6.1 Complaints

Solicitors may be the recipient of complaints, especially in those areas of law that are quite emotional or stressful for clients. For example the Legal Ombudsman's statistics show that family law, residential conveyancing and wills and probate are areas that receive the highest number of complaints. These are all areas of law where the consumer is seeking advice about a personal matter. At the other end of the spectrum commercial conveyancing receives very few complaints. This is the wrong forum to discuss the mechanics of the complaints process; suffice to say it is important for solicitors to treat their clients fairly where complaints arise as the first stage of the complaint process is dealt with by the firm. Indeed, the Code of Conduct O(1.11) states that complaints should be dealt with "promptly, fairly, openly and effectively". There is a heightened need for ethical thinking when dealing with situations where something might have gone wrong.

6.2 What is a complaint?

The SRA defines a complaint as:

> *"An oral or written expression of dissatisfaction which alleges that the complainant has suffered (or may suffer) financial loss, distress, inconvenience or other detriment".*

LeO adopts this definition as well, given that they are the body that deals with client complaints.

The first ethical dilemma is when to differentiate between a complaint and a grumble. This is a judgement call by the person who hears the complaint; in the first instance this might not be a fee earner but someone in a supporting role.

Some expressions of dissatisfaction may be easy to resolve in the moment - for example, if a client complains about their telephone call not being returned then an apology and explanation may suffice. Not every expression of dissatisfaction requires a full investigation.

A person who hears an expression of dissatisfaction can respond in a number of ways depending on their role within the firm, their training and of course their ethical viewpoint. For example, a receptionist at a busy firm may hear several clients per day complaining that they haven't had their calls returned. The receptionist may be untrained in referring complaints to the relevant person and they may also take the view the matter has nothing to do with them. Their approach could be described as "amoral" as they have no view on the complaints that are made.

That same receptionist may say that all clients complain because they are expecting a "Rolls Royce service for the price of a Lada!". This is a phrase that is often heard - there is sometimes a belief that clients shouldn't expect a platinum plated service if they are paying low prices. Of course, this is not reflected in the Code of Conduct.

A similar receptionist with a highly developed ethical sense will report every complaint to the relevant person so that the complaints process can be invoked. There are ethical judgements to be made every day by people who are not qualified solicitors, but should be trained to recognise and refer issues onward.

6.3 The framework for dealing with complaints

The main SRA Principles concerned with complaints are:

- Principle 4: You must act in the best interests of each client;

- Principle 5: You must provide a proper standard of service to your clients;

- Principle 7: You must comply with your legal and regulatory obligations and deal with your regulators and ombudsmen in an open, timely and co-operative manner.

Other Principles may need to be considered but these will depend on the specifics of the actual complaint.

There are 16 mandatory Outcomes that cover the areas of:

- Dealing with your client's matter;

- Accepting and refusing instructions;

- Information about costs;

- Complaints handling.

Client care and complaints is one of the more prescriptive and onerous areas of the SRA rules, although this is likely to change in the coming years. If the SRA successfully reduces the length of the Code of Conduct to 20 pages, these issues will be left to the firm to deal with. Although this area is more likely to be governed by a rules-based ethics approach, it should be noted that sometimes this results in an anti-ethical result.

A knock-on effect of having a more rules-based approach now is that it is more compliance orientated and potentially there is less scope for ethical judgement. One of the major reasons for this area being more prescriptive is that it is an area where the client's interests and the solicitor's interests can diverge.

6.4   Main areas for client complaints

Client complaints usually arise from a breakdown in communication between the solicitor and the client. The onus is on the solicitor to manage the relationship to ensure that an open communication channel always exists between themselves and their client and the client has a good understanding of the matter and its consequences.

During the progress of a matter, client complaints come from three main areas:

- Service standards;

- Costs information;

- The client's ability to make an informed decision based on the information provided by their solicitor.

6.5   Client service

The main issues for client service are clarity and managing client expectations. There are a total of 12 Indicative Behaviours which govern this area. As a result of the proliferation of rules, solicitors should present a client with terms of business before they proceed to engage in any work and manage client expectations.

In these terms of business and accompanying letters the firm needs to set out the scope of the matter they will deal with, define what is in and out of scope and discuss the foreseeable outcomes and knock-on effects. There is a huge amount of prescriptive information which is generally pre-designed within firms so that this isn't forgotten. The problem areas can be when the service standards expected are not met by the firm.

Many complaints upheld by the Legal Ombudsman are that the solicitor has failed to reply or that they have failed to follow instructions. It is difficult to understand why the solicitor would do this but these actions often result in compensatory awards being levied against the firm. The failure to follow instructions is obviously not a level of service that any firm aspires to.

Scenario: Lying to cover oversight

Facts

A client gives his solicitor instructions to issue an application in a neighbour dispute. The solicitor delays in making the application and does not issue proceedings, despite specific instructions to do so. When the client chases the solicitor, the solicitor says that he is waiting for the court to issue the application. The solicitor doesn't tell the client that the application has not been sent to the court as a result of his oversight, even though this is the truth. The client telephones the court and discovers that the application has not been received by the court and raises the matter as a complaint with the firm.

Rules

Principle 2: Act with integrity.

Principle 4: Act in the best interests of each client.

Principle 5: Provide a proper standard of service to your clients.

Principle 6: Behave in a way that maintains the trust the public places in you and in the provision of legal services.

Potential ethical issues/professional breaches

Lying to a client to cover up wrongdoing is both ethically wrong and a regulatory breach. It is not acting in the best interests of the client to mislead them about their case, particularly as this is an example of failure to provide a good level of service. A solicitor could be accused of dishonesty and if this was proven, the SDT could strike that solicitor off. Once again, any attempt to cover up the poor service issue is ethically worse than the poor service issue itself. The regulatory penalty is much higher for the latter behaviour.

Possible approaches

It is much better for the solicitor to admit that the client's instructions haven't been followed and offer immediate correction, apology and even compensation. If the firm attempts to restrict the right of the client to go to LeO to seek redress, the firm could find itself involved in a bigger mess. Firms are not permitted to restrict the client from approaching LeO and to attempt to impose such a restriction could be viewed as professional negligence. The SRA would view this action as an attempt to take advantage of a third party and would impose penalties for doing so.

Suggested reaction/steps to avoid

Don't mislead the client about steps that have/have not been taken in accordance with their instructions. Do not attempt to restrict the right of the client to approach LeO even if it is part of the firm's attempt to resolve matters.

The best way to ensure that the client doesn't go to LeO after a complaint is received is to offer restitution that the client is happy with. If this is done, then the client will not feel the need to approach LeO about this issue.

6.6 Costs information

Alongside scoping out the nature of the work to be undertaken the solicitor must give an outline of what the matter is expected to cost. The client must also be made aware of the potential financial liabilities they may incur if the matter goes against them.

There are a number of ways in which costs information may be deficient or the cause of a complaint:

(1) No costs information is given to the client at all. This is not compliant with the rules and certainly doesn't hold the profession in a good light.

(2) Broad costs information is given, which is linked to an hourly rate but this isn't updated and by the end of the case this is wrong. This is not compliant with the rules and doesn't hold the profession in a good light.

(3) A quote is given for a fixed fee but the firm seeks to depart from this agreement during the retainer due to unforeseen circumstances. The firm should have been clear about the scope of the fixed fee from the outset. It would be wrong to renege on a fixed fee quote and would amount to a substantiated complaint of poor service.

(4) A quote is given for a fixed fee which has no bearing on the complexity of the case or the hours that would be spent on the case; for example, if the work was straightforward form filling and the client is charged on a fixed fee 10 times what the hourly rate would be.

Scenario: Inadequate costs information

Facts

The client complains about the fact that the solicitor has given inadequate costs information and the matter is investigated by the relevant person (not the fee earner). The solicitor who reviews the file

119

likes the fee earner and has always held them in high regard. However, the file is not in great order and shows that costs information has been scant and not properly updated throughout the matter.

Rules

Principle 5: Provide a proper standard of service to your clients.

Outcome (1.13): Clients receive the best possible information, both at the time of engagement and when appropriate as their matter progresses, about the likely overall cost of their matter.

Potential ethical issues/professional breaches

Not only is there a regulatory requirement to keep the client informed about their costs, it is ethically right to do so. Clients should know what they are being charged so they can make an informed decision as to whether to use your firm's services or not. Without good information at the outset, the client's decision-making is hindered and this does not produce an ethical result. For example, estate agents often quote high selling prices for houses in order to secure a contract and defend their own high rates. It is not ethical for them to do this knowing that the information is false or unclear. The same principles apply in the legal environment.

Possible approaches

The supervising solicitor could overrule the complaint on the basis that the solicitor is usually good at giving this information and this is just an oversight. This is not in the best interests of this particular client who hasn't received the best costs information. This would be in the best interests of the firm and the individual solicitor in the short term. In the longer term, the firm might get a reputation (as some estate agents have) of quoting low and charging high which means that people will stop relying on their costs estimates and may stop approaching the firm at all. The individual solicitor will feel that their approach to costs information has been sanctioned by the firm and may continue in the same vein in the future. This may then encourage poor practice within the firm - a bad apple is turning the barrel bad.

A client who is fobbed off in this manner may approach LeO, the firm will pay the flat fee of £400 and may face a compensatory payment to the client. The loss of money and fee earning time in dealing with the complaint with LeO will be considerable.

Suggested reaction/steps to avoid

A better approach, which is more reflective of the Principles and the Code of Conduct, would be to recognise the fault and offer the client a reduction in their bill. Apologising to the client may also be appropriate.

The solicitor should be given further training on the issue of costs information and the need to provide it accurately. This approach would address both short and long term issues. If the client was still unhappy with the level of redress and escalated their complaint to LeO, the complaint would be investigated but if they considered the resolution offered was reasonable, the flat fee of £400 would be waived.

6.7 Making an informed decision

Ultimately it is down to the ability of the client, based on the information provided, to make an informed decision about the matter in hand, how it will be dealt with and by whom, and the scope of the options available to them in how to proceed as to whether they will complain or not. Clients will always be disappointed if a matter does not end favourably for them but the solicitor can take much preventative action so that the client does not blame them no matter what the outcome. If the solicitor is careful in advising the client to enable them to make choices during the proceedings, it is more difficult for the client to blame the solicitor for the outcome.

6.8 Complaints handling

Principle 7: Comply with your legal and regulatory obligations and deal with your regulators and ombudsmen in an open, timely and co-operative manner

The solicitor is obliged to inform the client from the outset that they are governed by the Legal Ombudsman Service and to outline how the client can bring any complaints they may have to them. Failure to meet this requirement is an immediate breach which will be sanctioned. A well run firm will include all this information within the terms and conditions of business or client care letter.

Dealing with the complaint internally

IB(1.22) outlines that every firm should have a written complaints procedure that is referred to at the outset of the matter and is available upon any request from the client. From a regulatory perspective the most important stipulations are that complaints are dealt with promptly and fairly with sufficient investigation of the circumstances.

It is important that someone independent investigates the complaint and that they have sufficient power to come to an independent conclusion. There should be a transparent methodology for documenting the complaint, gathering the evidence and documenting the logic used to make the final decision.

If the firm appoints the person who had primary control of the file to investigate the complaint, it might not be considered to be a fair investigation by the client. This is an ethical consideration for the firm to take into account - many people would not believe that the fee earner could have sufficient objectivity to investigate a complaint against them.

If the complaint is then raised with the Legal Ombudsman, the firm should co-operate fully and transparently in an effort to get the complaint satisfactorily resolved in the swiftest manner possible.

Solicitors and firms should behave in a professional manner throughout the period of the complaint and should note that the client can also complain to the SRA for issues such as excessive rudeness.

Scenario: Backdated attendance note

Facts

The client complains that the solicitor hasn't given advice on a particular issue and they raise the matter as a complaint. The solicitor needs to identify the issue as a complaint and activate the complaints process. The solicitor knows that if the client goes to LeO then they will ask to see evidence of the advice given to the client which will be in the form of written advice or a note of oral advice given to the client. The solicitor is sure that they gave advice to the client orally about the matter but there is no evidence on the file to support that. The solicitor decides to backdate an attendance note to support the advice that they believe they have given, believing that they could not get caught doing this. Furthermore, whilst the attendance note might be backdated, the advice was given.

Rules

Principle 2: Act with integrity.

Principle 4: Act in the best interests of each client.

Principle 5: Provide a proper standard of service to your clients.

Principle 6: Behave in a way that maintains the trust the public places in you and in the provision of legal services.

Principle 7: The firm would need to cooperate with LeO if the complaint went to them.

Indicative Behaviour (1.22): The firm should have a complaints procedure that is disclosed to the client.

Potential ethical issues/professional breaches

Even if the solicitor did give the relevant advice to the client, back-dating evidence of this is professional misconduct. It is not in keeping with Principle 4, which requires the solicitor to act in the best interests of the client. The solicitor cannot rely on their memory of advice that was given orally - only an attendance note made contemporaneously would be good evidence. It is even better if the solicitor follows up oral advice with written confirmation to the client, for the avoidance of doubt. The failure to keep good records of the telephone advice is not in keeping with Principle 5 as it does not provide a good standard of service to the client and does not reflect well on the firm or the profession.

Ethically, it lacks integrity to manufacture a document to prevent a complaint being made. It is a short term fix as the act of creating the document is a more serious breach than the issue of poor service.

Possible approaches

The solicitor should admit the oversight and make amends to the client. If no detriment has been caused by the failure to advise then a compensatory offer should be made to the client to reflect the poor service element. The firm will save time and costs of a LeO investigation by reaching an agreement with the client. LeO charges firms £400 for every complaint it investigates and this is borne in mind when an offer of settlement is made.

Suggested reaction/steps to avoid

It is not advisable to make up attendance notes, emails or letters to circumvent a complaint from a client. Not only are there serious regulatory concerns, it is unethical to do so. Taking this route could lead to a solicitor being struck off for committing a dishonesty offence. The act of covering up poor service is a worse regulatory breach than the poor service element.

6.9 Negligence

The circumstances that give rise to a complaint of poor service and a claim in negligence can often be the same set of circumstances. It may be that the client feels the level of compensation they are looking for will not be provided by LeO and they therefore may decide it is appropriate to bring a claim in negligence. LeO will not look at a complaint where a negligence claim has been initiated. However, they can look at the complaint first and as long as the client does not accept their resolution, the client can still raise a claim in negligence.

The governing Principle in this area is Principle 5: Provide a proper standard of service to your clients.

The relevant Outcome is O(1.5): the service you provide client is competent, delivered in a timely manner and takes into account your client's needs and circumstances

Occasionally, reporting a solicitor to the professional body may not provide sufficient monetary or disciplinary remedy for the client's circumstances so they may have to resort to bringing the solicitor to court for negligence or breach of contract. Whilst this might address the monetary complaint, disciplinary sanctions are imposed by professional bodies and not the court. Sometimes, a client can feel that the sanctions imposed by the professional bodies to do not remedy the wrong that they have suffered and then they take the matter further.

Normally it is quite easy to establish whether a contract is in place as the solicitor would have supplied the client with terms and conditions before starting the matter. Sometimes there can be ambiguous scenarios, such as third parties relying on a solicitor's advice, where you need to establish whether a contract is in place or not. If there is no contract in place between the solicitor and the "client" then no court proceedings for negligence can take place.

6.10 What are the principles of negligence?

In order for a client to show that a solicitor was negligent there must be three elements present:

(1)   The solicitor owed a duty of care;

(2)   The solicitor breached that duty of care; and

(3)   The client suffered a loss as a result of a breach of that duty.

Proving negligence is usually a rules-based approach, with a few ethical issues that arise.

6.11   Does the solicitor owe a duty of care?

There are three factors that need to be assessed when considering whether a duty of care is owed which are foreseeability, proximity and justice and reasonableness.

(1)   The foreseeability test is whether it was foreseeable that the solicitor might harm their client by their actions;

(2)   The proximity test measures whether the two parties were close, either physically or in a relationship;

(3)   The justice and reasonableness test is whether is it just and reasonable to impose a duty of care.

If it can be shown that a client relationship exists then it is easy to prove a duty of care. It is more difficult where this relationship is in doubt or does not exist.

6.12   Duty of care to third parties

Normally a solicitor gives advice to a client in the knowledge that the advice is only for them and not to be relied upon by third parties. There are some situations where third parties do place reliance on advice given to another party such as the beneficiaries of a will. In these scenarios the solicitor must be able to reasonably deduce that the advice will be relied upon by specific third parties. A client telling a separate third party about advice given by a solicitor, where the solicitor has no knowledge of that third party, will not establish a duty of care.

6.13   Breach of duty of due care and skill

To show that a solicitor has breached their duty of due care and skill the solicitor has to be shown to have exercised a lower level of due care and skill than that of a reasonable solicitor in that situation. It is also vital to show that the solicitor showed a lack of due care and skill in relation to the scope of their retainer. The retainer should have been set out before or at the point the solicitor accepted instructions to act.

It is also important to note that a solicitor cannot be found negligent for merely losing a case. However, in matters where there is a definitive objective which is within the means of a reasonably competent solicitor, and where it is reasonable to assume that the solicitor has control of the outcome, such as the drafting of a will, non-production or defective production of the final outcome can lead to a claim of negligence.

6.14   Is a solicitor culpable for lack of knowledge of the law?

Due to the depth, breadth and complexity of the law and its ever evolving nature there is no way that solicitors would be expected to have an in depth knowledge of all of it. However, if they do not have a sufficient level of knowledge in that area to provide their client with a sufficient level of due care and skill then they need to research those areas or defer to another legal expert in the particular field in question. We have explored the solicitor's obligation to maintain their competence to practise in the context of the new Competence Statement in Chapter 2: Rules-based ethics.

Lack of knowledge of the law is looked upon dimly by the courts. However, the advice given by a solicitor has to be judged upon its reasonableness at the time. If a solicitor acts or gives advice in what is seen to be standard at the time then they will be deemed not to be negligent. However, this standard has to be free of foreseeable and/or avoidable risk.

If a solicitor can show that they reasonably followed the SRA Code of Conduct and good practice as it relates to that Code, it would be highly unlikely that a court would find a solicitor to be negligent.

6.15 Complex cases and specialist lawyers

If a solicitor gets involved in a matter and then discovers that more specialist legal knowledge than they can provide is required, should the solicitor declare this to the client and excuse themselves? Ethically, it is the right thing to do to admit that one's knowledge is insufficient and refer the matter onwards or acquire the knowledge required in order to complete the matter.

In matters where the legal points are complex and the solicitor does not hold themselves out to be an expert in these points they would need to show they sought a Counsel's or expert's advice or both. Not to do so would open themselves up to accusations of negligence were the matter not to proceed favourably for their client. Ethical decision-making that goes wrong could end up with an action for negligence.

Another related point would be that work needs to be allocated to a person of suitable standing and expertise to complete the work to the professional standard the matter deserves. If overly complex work is given to a trainee or junior member of staff without adequate supervision or support the firm could open themselves up to a negligence claim.

6.16 Can a lawyer be found negligent for not following the instructions of a client?

This very much depends on the circumstances of the matter. If the client gave a reasonable legal instruction that was within the capabilities of the solicitor then, nine times out of ten, if the solicitor did not carry out that instruction they would be negligent. However, clients don't always give reasonable, actionable, legal or ethical instructions.

Scenario: Deceiving clients

Facts

The client instructed the solicitor to proceed with litigation in circumstances where the solicitor did not think the client would win. The client did not agree to proceed with ADR processes despite good advice to do so. The solicitor deceived the client into believing that proceedings had been issued when they had not. The solicitor had hoped that the client would negotiate a settlement rather than issue proceedings. The client discovered the deception and complained.

The firm apologised and offered remedies which were accepted by the client and no negligence action was taken.

The solicitor agreed that he should have been more firm with the client about issuing the proceedings against his advice, rather than lie to the client in the hope that he would negotiate a settlement.

What the solicitor needs to do is to inform and advise the client of the possible courses of action and the reasonable expectable consequences of action or inaction. Once the solicitor is satisfied that their advice has been understood by the client it is the client's decision as to the course of action to take. The solicitor has to then make the ethical decision whether they can carry out the client's instructions or refuse to act. If the solicitor refuses to act then they need to document the exact circumstances and reasoning they undertook when they decided not to act.

6.17 Can a solicitor be found negligent for advice given in relation to settlements?

A solicitor can only give reasonable advice based on the circumstances of the case and making a professional judgement on what spectrum of results the client should expect. Therefore if a solicitor can show that they exercised reasonable due care and skill when giving the advice on the amount a client should settle for, for example, a client cannot say they were negligent if the final settlement is lower. Ethically, the solicitor needs to ensure that the reason that they are encouraging a settlement is in the best interests of the client. If there are overwhelming personal reasons that the solicitor is encouraging settlement then this would be ethically wrong.

> ### Scenario: Encouraging settlement
>
> **Facts**
>
> The settlement figure to the client is £100,000 with costs to the firm of £25,000. The solicitor knows that the costs figure is probably higher than they would get outside the terms of the offer but that the settlement figure for the client should possibly be £125,000. The solicitor should not encourage settlement just to get the higher fees that are on offer.

6.18 Following the advice of a barrister

If a solicitor is following the advice of a barrister are they absolved of any claims of negligence? Again, it largely revolves around the circumstances of the case and the balance of knowledge between the two individuals. If it is a complex case in a specialist area of law and the barrister is such a specialist, then it would be reasonable that any claims of negligence should fall solely on the barrister. But in no circumstances does the solicitor get off scot-free. The solicitor must always apply reasonable care and judgement to any advice they may receive from a barrister to ensure that it is fair and relevant to their client and subsequently the best course of action to follow.

6.19 Wasted costs orders

Is it ethical for a solicitor to pursue an action that they know is doomed to failure or is an action that will only incur costs for the other side? These types of action can be known as:

(a) nuisance claims; or

(b) speculative claims; or

(c) vexatious claims.

Sometimes the claims are made with the intent of securing a settlement rather than the paying party incurring disproportionate legal costs. There are two instances where this would occur.

(1) Where the client instructs the solicitor to pursue the order (in spite of advice to the contrary);

(2) Where the solicitor advises the client to pursue the order (costs proportionality would need to be taken into account).

Some solicitors might take the view that it is his or her job to outline options to the client. Ultimately, the decision of how to proceed is for the client and not the solicitor. In this scenario, the law recognises that the solicitor has a duty to third parties.

According to Section 51(7) of the Senior Courts Act 1981:

""wasted costs" means any costs incurred by a party:

(a) as a result of any improper, unreasonable or negligent act or omission on the part of any legal or other representative or any employee of such a representative; or

(b) which, in the light of any such act or omission occurring after they were incurred, the court considers it is unreasonable to expect that party to pay".

Therefore, if the court deems the application improper, unreasonable or negligent then the court may hold that the solicitor who brought the case is liable for all or part of the incurred costs.

At this point the interests of the solicitor and their client would diverge as the section is meant to act as a deterrent to prevent unnecessary applications. A solicitor should therefore make an ethical decision regarding an application before the risk of a wasted cost order arises, and advise their client accordingly.

6.20 Summary

It is inevitable that a client may reach the end of proceedings and feel that their experience has not been as expected. Professionals should be subjected to an external and objective complaints procedure and even negligence claims for the work they do. If we were told that we could never complain about the service of the medical professional we would feel very vulnerable.

There are ethical dimensions to complaints or negligence actions and solicitors should try to be objective when dealing with them. They should do their best to rectify any areas where it is agreed that service has not been as expected. Clearly, covering up a complaint, failing to deal with it or dealing with it rudely does the reputation of the firm and the profession no good.

Chapter 7: Ethics and social media

7.1 Introduction

It is very difficult to associate the idea of sites such as Facebook and Twitter as having any relevance to legal regulation and professional ethics. However, the technological developments in electronic communication have dragged the legal profession kicking and screaming into the 21st century.

The Law Society defines social media as:

> *"websites and applications that enable users to create and share content or to participate in social networking...*
>
> *Social media are web-based and mobile technologies that turn communication into active dialogue. There are many different types of social media channels which attract specific audiences for different purposes."*

Essentially social media is any form of online application that allows its users to, publicly or otherwise, share information amongst networks they are connected to, or even to the public in general. Social media sites can often be accessed in a variety of ways, be it by way of an internet browser or through an application on a tablet or mobile device.

Some practitioners less familiar with the concept of social media may raise an eyebrow about the relevance of a chapter regarding social media in a handbook about the professional ethics of solicitors in practice. Consider, however, that from a marketing perspective social media is an increasingly popular and effective way of expanding a firm's marketing and networking circles and communicating the firm's ethos to a wide range of individuals.

Readers who have a firm understanding of social media may want to skip to section 7.6 which discusses the ethics of utilising social media

This is leading firms and solicitors to use social media more and more. As a result of this increased use in social media, solicitors are quickly becoming acutely aware (and some learning the hard way) that their online interactions are subject to the regulatory and ethical principles of the profession in equal measures to their offline interactions. This has been particularly evident from recent disciplinary events in the media.

Most firms are now accepting that social media has evolved beyond a tool purely utilised for networking personally to become powerful marketing devices for both firms themselves and also the individual solicitors within those firms. It is now considered commonplace for law firms to have their own Twitter and Facebook pages to the extent that consumers can often associate the lack of an online presence as somewhat of a warning sign.

Social media has been witnessing an explosion of use by solicitors' firms since around 2011, but it is only recently that the majority of firms have embraced the potential rewards it offers. Equally, individual solicitors have understood that social media offers an easy way for them to develop their own separate online identity, independent from their firm. Compared to other industries, the application of social media by the legal profession is relatively in its infancy and a new mechanism of marketing being explored. As a result of this relative infancy, lawyers have been extremely reticent to fully appreciate the application of professional ethical issues to their interactions online, and in particular, through social media. The key issue for solicitors who use social media regularly is that the Code of Conduct will apply to their actions, regardless of whether they are at work or "off the clock" in their own personal time. The last thing on most solicitor's minds after a few drinks on a Saturday night is the Code of Conduct!

This chapter will seek to discuss the ethical and regulatory issues which apply to the online interactions of solicitors both in a professional and personal capacity, and discuss actions which can be taken to ensure that this exposure is limited.

7.2   The rise of social media and online interactions

The rapid expansion of the legal profession's use of social media and electronic communication should not come as a surprise. The benefits of electronic communication are well known and we do not propose to have great levels of discussion regarding this; very few practitioners will now solely send correspondence by way of letter as a result of the widespread use of email. Social media operates on the same wavelength and offers many professional and personal benefits to both a firm and individual solicitors in that firm.

7.3   Social media in the legal profession

It is important to remember that in its infancy, social media was used primarily for online interactions between individuals, purely for the purpose of socialisation; it was not until social media sites began to possess serious traction that social media was properly utilised for business purposes. It was even later that the legal profession began to understand its significant benefits.

Social media is typically used by solicitors in two ways:

(1)   **A marketing tool for the firm**. A nominated individual, or the firm's marketing department, may use social media sites as a way of promoting the firm to the general public. This is done in a variety of ways, for example:

- Posting about the firm's objectives;

- Providing an insight into the firm's ethos and practice style;

- Offering comments on the changing legal landscape;

- Posting photographs of their employees engaging with the local community (such as charity events hosted by the firm);

- Posting "offers", such as particular fixed fee packages for example;

- Posting links to the firm's "blog" for potential clients to consider.

(2) **A marketing tool for the individual solicitor**. An individual solicitor may use social media as a way of establishing and promoting their own services, or for their own private reasons unrelated to professional promotion. Whilst an individual solicitor may utilise their social media accounts to promote the services of the firm they are currently employed by, they will also be promoting their identity and offerings independently of the firm by using social media. In a similar way to how a firm might operate a social media account, individual solicitors will often promote themselves and their firms in the following ways:

- Publishing comments and blogs on developments in their individual practice areas;

- Posting photographs of their "extra-curricular" activities;

- Engaging with other firms and practitioners;

- Interacting with clients (albeit less common).

Individual solicitors may not consciously promote either themselves or their firms through the use of social media and many simply comment on areas of law through these platforms out of curiosity, and without self-promotion in mind. Additionally, many individual solicitors will use social media for personal reasons and interactions, with absolutely no professional intentions in mind. It is therefore necessary to differentiate between different accounts for individual solicitors:

- **Professional accounts**: these will be accounts where solicitors use social media for the purpose of promoting their services or the services of the firm. These accounts will tend to post content publicly, and will contain mostly professional posts regarding their own practice areas or content which promotes their or their firm's personal ethos and practice style.

- **Personal accounts**: personal accounts conversely will be accounts which solicitors use for non-professional purposes, such as corresponding with friends and family and keeping their networks updated on more personal updates like holidays and relationships. These accounts tend to be private and viewable only by those people the solicitor has authorised to view their private network (e.g. their friends).

We will see that certain platforms of social media will lend themselves more towards personal accounts and others will lend themselves more towards professional matters.

To complicate matters even further, some solicitors will not appreciate that there is a distinction to be had between these two forms of use, and will often use one for both professional and personal accounts, which, as we will see, can lead to complications.

7.4   The benefits of social media

We will briefly consider the potential benefits that social media offers to firms and individual solicitors, although you may be aware of many of these.

- Social media raises the profile of the firm and individuals for little or no cost regardless of the size of the firm in question. Even the smallest of firms will be able to appoint an individual (albeit under supervision) to promote the firm by way of social media. Unlike traditional advertising the basic functions of most social media sites are free and therefore, other than any business overheads, the cost of social media compared to more traditional methods is refreshingly cost effective. In any event, even where firms subscribe to paid advertisements on social media, the costs of social media campaigns compared to traditional print campaigns are inherently minimal and are much more likely to reach a wider audience.

- Social media provides an opportunity for the firm to determine what information is available online about both itself and other solicitors, rather than relying on the word of mouth of third parties. For example, legal recruiters now have the benefit of LinkedIn to search for profiles of solicitors, allowing them to trawl through various solicitor profiles and match potential suitors to their client's needs. Equally, firms can do this where they require a particular solicitor for a role, allowing them to head-hunt candidates effectively.

- Most social media sites allow posts to be directed to individual people or target audiences, provided that particular market possesses an online presence. This allows the ethos and sales pitches of the firm that are communicated by way of social media to be specifically directed at the desired market of the firm, ensuring marketing campaigns reach their intended audiences. This is a significant improvement over the more "scatter-gun" approach of traditional marketing.

- In a world dominated by the use of the internet, many clients will expect firms to possess an online presence and to interact by way of electronic communication. In the same way as you may express some concern over an opponent firm which possesses no website, many clients will consider a lack of online and social media presence as somewhat of a red flag. An online presence and ability to market the firm effectively by social media suggests that the firm possesses a very forward thinking attitude and is able to adapt to evolution and change.

- Social media removes the constraints of geographical barriers that more traditional marketing simply cannot achieve; online posts and marketing can be targeted towards markets that the firm previously could not reach. This is particularly useful for firms with specialisms in niche practice areas as they are able to specifically communicate and advertise their services nationally, attracting clients who may never have been aware of the firm in the absence of social media.

7.5　The risks of social media

Whilst the benefits of social media are many, the ability to quickly communicate content to a wide public audience does of course carry with it a large amount of risk, particularly from the perspective of professional regulation.

- Solicitors are by their very nature very vocal about areas of law they are passionate about; it is a requirement of the job! When combined with the instantaneous nature of social media, any rash comments, particularly where untruthful, could lead to liability for both the firm and the individual solicitor in tort for some form of defamation. Equally, boisterous or unsubstantiated claims made on social media have the potential to mislead the public, a breach of Outcome (8.1).

- More seriously, any posts which could be considered to breach the regulatory principles, such as the duty to act with integrity, could easily attract the disciplinary attention of the SRA. If anything, social media is more likely to attract the attention of the SRA given that it is publicly made available and permanent, meaning even where a person regrets a post and deletes it is not always the case that the message has not already been seen by others and recorded in some way.

- It is all too easy to indirectly and inadvertently make the private affairs of a client (over which solicitors owe a duty of confidentiality) public by way of social media. As we will see this can easily occur through inferences drawn from social media posts, even where the solicitor does not intend it to occur.

- The risks of social media apply not only to you, but also your clients. Your client's social media posts can be produced as evidence in litigation. It would, for example, be difficult for you to maintain a personal injury claim for reduced mobility if your opponents are able to adduce photographic evidence of your client's recent skiing holiday from their Facebook page. It is therefore advisable to warn your client about making information available which might compromise their case in some way.

- The removal of geographical barriers also carries with it some element of risk. Of course it carries the firm to markets it hasn't previously had access to; however this also presents an element of danger where the firm does not understand the market it is entering into. Particularly where these new markets are international, the risk of misunderstanding market elements through social media posts could cause offence, and may raise certain diversity issues.

- Whilst firms can place controls on their employees' social media usage regarding what they can and cannot utilise social media accounts for whilst under the firm's employment, ultimately if an employee does post something irresponsible, unprofessional or unethical, it can undermine the firm's image and expose a risk to its integrity. Whilst the firm can take disciplinary proceedings against their employee for this, the damage done to the firm may well already have been spread potentially globally and even if the employee deletes the post, it may well already have been permanently captured or commented upon by a third party.

7.6   The ethics of social media

The interactions of solicitors on social media, both during office hours and outside them, presents multiple ethical dilemmas for solicitors. It is often difficult for solicitors to appreciate this because social media is fairly new to the legal profession, and therefore many solicitors struggle to take it seriously when contemplating Code of Conduct breaches. As a result of this solicitors rarely contemplate ethics and regulatory conduct when utilising social media; most solicitors think of serious ethical issues as including only accounts breaches or serious criminal actions.

After all, how on earth could putting something on Facebook result in a striking off?

7.7　Why do ethics apply to social media?

The risks of social media can be contextualised by comparing the issues to that of the interaction between lawyers and the "traditional" media, which has long sat uneasily alongside the profession.

Lord Woolfe has previously suggested that parties to litigation and their respective solicitors should not make comments to the media in reference to ongoing litigation without the express leave of the court. His reasoning behind this was that he argued that the parties were entitled to have their issues determined before the court without "improper interference with the course of justice"[9]. We should assume that the same dicta applies equally to statements that have been issued by solicitors through social media. Statements made online by solicitors have the capacity to be perceived by the public and the media to carry authority even where the content of that statement is completely inaccurate. As Lord Woolfe stated:

> *"The professionalism and sense of duty to legal advisers who conduct litigation of this nature should mean that the courts are able to rely on the legal advisers to exercise great self-restraint when making comment [to the media]…"*

In considering this statement it is easy to see how the risk of communication between solicitors and the wider public on an instantaneous platform could result in ethical and regulatory breaches. Simply put, social media makes it a lot easier for inappropriate or accidental comments made by solicitors to be communicated on a mass basis. If, for example, a solicitor makes an inappropriate comment on their social media account regarding ongoing proceedings then there is a real risk that they will prejudice current or anticipated proceedings, undermining the authority of the court and the trust in the profession.

Of course, the risk of professional breaches in the context of social media is not restricted to matters involving ongoing litigation; in theory any of the SRA principles can be breached, often unwittingly, by a solicitor utilising social media. As we have previously seen, this is also complicated by the fact that many solicitors will combine their professional and private social media accounts, blurring the boundaries between what is a personal interaction on social media and what is a professional one. Solicitors may be surprised to learn that unethical posts on their private social media accounts made outside of work hours can still be considered regulatory breaches by the SRA.

In considering how regulatory ethics applies to social media it may assist you to consider the following sections of the SRA Code of Conduct:

---

[9] *Hodgson v Imperial Tobacco Limited [1998] EWCA Civ 224*

(1)   Chapter 1 - client care;

(2)   Chapter 4 - confidentiality and disclosure;

(3)   Chapter 8 - publicity;

(4)   Chapter 11 - relations with third parties.

Whilst it is perfectly possible in theory to breach any of the mandatory Principles, the Principles that are the most likely to be tested when an individual is engaged in social media activity are:

(1)   Principle 2 - You must act with integrity;

(2)   Principle 3 - You must not allow your independence to be compromised;

(3)   Principle 4 - You must act in the client's best interests;

(4)   Principle 6 - You must behave in a way that maintains the trust the public places in you and in the provision of legal services.

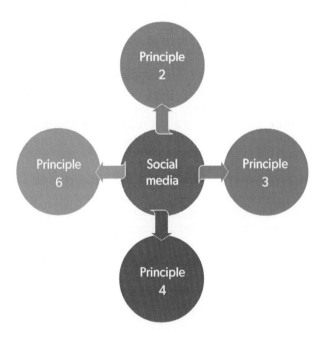

Fig 28: Social media and the regulatory Principles

Of these Principles it is Principles 2 and 6 which are most easily breached by solicitors through social media.

It is also extremely important that ethics are applied to social media due to the speed at which content can not only be posted, but also shared. Controversial posts have known to become "viral" (that is they are shared between multiple networks extremely quickly, and ultimately to thousands of site users) within hours of the post being made. Social media is therefore particularly dangerous to an individual solicitor, a firm and the profession as a whole because it is a public forum where anything can become accessible to thousands of people extremely quickly, and the record will be permanent.

It can often seem somewhat bizarre to suggest, but in the most serious of breaches of the Code of Conduct, a solicitor could face being struck off the roll as a result of their actions. Being struck off the roll for an absent minded post on a social media site may seem ludicrous, but where the post is a serious breach of professional conduct this may well be the appropriate sanction. Consider for example that whilst most people may not consider not paying for a train ticket anything serious, because of the dishonesty status of this offence, solicitors have been struck off for this.

Above all, social media remains such a significant risk for solicitors purely because its novelty means that it appears to be innocuous. However, remember at all times that social media is a public forum, and where comments are made in that forum they can be communicated to other networks with frightening speed.

7.8 The importance of social media in the legal profession

Despite this and given the benefits of social media it is not surprising that the legal profession has been quick to monetise upon the benefits it offers. But why is social media so important to the legal profession, and why should we even consider ethical principles when utilising it?

The main reason behind the importance of social media is that it allows solicitors to engage with their colleagues, other solicitors and even the judiciary, allowing instantaneous mass debate on topics such as law reforms or changes to court services. This collaboration between various legal professionals, particularly those who practice in areas affected by reforms, is an excellent way for the profession to collaborate with one another. For example, forums on LinkedIn allow its users to discuss and comment upon the developments in practice. Before the advent of social media, outside of large scale meetings of practitioners, this was not possible with such ease and transparency.

It may seem extreme, but the widespread use of social media by the legal profession is now helping to shape how the rule of law evolves; as social media is an instantaneous platform for commentary and debate on the changing legal environment it can be suggested that it acts like a pulse for how the profession perceive certain legal issues.

7.9 Understanding different social media platforms

One key thing to understand about social media is that there are various social media sites available for practitioners to promote their businesses, and that all of these sites employ various different functions and privacy settings.

There are many types of social networks with which solicitors may engage during their careers; in a response to a recent SRA consultation one firm responded that it utilised as many as 16! Fortunately most firms are unlikely to use anywhere near that number. The majority of firms will use the more commonly known sites such as LinkedIn or Twitter. However, the social media sites which potentially could be of use in a law firm in order of relevance are:

- The firm's website
- LinkedIn
- Twitter
- Forums of legal debate
- YouTube
- Facebook

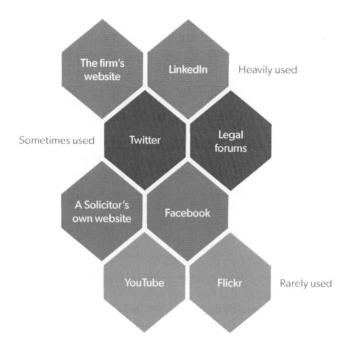

Fig 29: Types of social networks used by law firms

A crucial element of remaining ethically vigilant on social media is understanding that different social media sites employ different privacy options. You should also remember that just because a post is not made publicly available on one social media site does not mean that it is not publicly available on another! Equally, one site may well change their privacy settings, making private posts public, or vice versa.

This chapter focuses on the most common social media applications utilised by the legal profession; however, when utilising social media or any other form of online interaction, you should have the Principles of the Code of Conduct at the forefront of your mind.

7.10 Facebook

Most practitioners will be familiar with the social media site Facebook due to the fact it is one of the oldest and largest social media platforms available, with an almost universal recognition amongst the general public. Facebook has become so inoculated within the majority of the public's daily lives that phrases such as "send me a message" have been replaced with "Facebook me".

The popularity of Facebook means that law firms are likely to want to capitalise upon its large user network, and indeed Facebook certainly offers the possibility to do this. Businesses can set up their own "pages" (which are much like individual user profiles) that users of Facebook can follow (known as "liking a page") and receive posts from that page. It is now extremely common for law firms to have their own Facebook pages, which are used to post updates about the firm and its services.

The main issue with Facebook within the legal profession is that it bases its roots so firmly within private social interactions between individuals, and thus possesses a more relaxed environment which is considered detached from the world of professional regulation. After all, Facebook began its days as a site for Harvard University students to share updates on their lives between the Harvard networks. With this foundation in mind it is very difficult to see how Facebook has progressed to a marketing tool for solicitors.

Facebook is also increasingly dangerous because individuals automatically assume that the content they post on their Facebook account can only be viewed by their friends (i.e. other users who have been authorised to view content). This is an incorrect assumption; the default settings of Facebook are indeed such that only friends can see posts, but individuals who misunderstand the privacy settings can easily change settings, making posts they assume are private, public. Additionally, some parts of a user's profile will be viewable publicly by default, such as the profile picture selected by the user. It is important to recall that not only inappropriate words can cause issues on Facebook, but also photos.

The personal basis of Facebook is such that the network channels have evolved primarily for personal use, and as such their audiences are typically more responsive towards content that their friends have shared on their networks, rather than the business minded posts of law firms. This has the result that an individual posting photos of their recent holiday is likely to attract far more than a post by a solicitor's firm about the reforms of a particular legal sector.

Because of this firms tend to approach Facebook with caution. However, arguably the main concern with Facebook is its use by individual solicitors. Most solicitors will possess their own Facebook account, and utilise it purely for their personal interactions outside of work. The issue with this is that a solicitor using Facebook outside of the office may, by virtue of the private and relaxed nature of the site, completely forget that their professional obligations apply to this online environment, even if their posts are restricted to their "friends". Consider this example:

Scenario: Facebook post

Facts

You are a solicitor in a small High Street firm. You have just arrived home after a week-long trial for a particularly vulnerable client. Unfortunately the trial was not successful and judgment was made against your client, and the costs order is such that your client is likely to lose their home to pay for the costs. You feel that part of the reason you lost is because your opponent and their solicitors adduced key evidence extremely late, and were very bullish regarding the application to admit this at the trial out of time. After one too many glasses of wine you log into your Facebook account and post:

> *"Terrible time at the Royal Courts of Justice this week. Just goes to show that 99% of solicitors are corrupt and will do anything to win!"*

Whilst your profile settings are such that only your friends will see this post, what issues are there regarding this post?

Rules

Principle 2: Act with integrity.

Principle 4: Behave in a way which maintains the trust the public places in you and the provision of legal services.

Outcome (4.1): You keep the affairs of clients confidential unless disclosure is required or permitted by law or the client consents.

Potential ethical issues/professional breaches

The mistake in this scenario is to assume that purely because Facebook is a private social media site, and the solicitor is not at work, means that there are no regulatory breaches. This is not true. This post, when viewed by the friends of the solicitor, is extremely likely to damage the trust the public places in the provision of legal services.

Equally, consider that even though the message is private now, any member of the solicitor's network could copy the message and display it on a more public forum. On a side note, consider that mentioning that the case is at the RCJ could draw an inference to who you act for. If this post became public and the other firm were identified, you could potentially face proceedings for defamation.

Possible approaches

Delete the post and inform your compliance officer (even though you are not at work).

Maintain a policy of not posting negative comments about your job on your Facebook page.

Suggested reaction/steps to avoid

This is a scenario where the best advice is simply to maintain a policy against sharing content of this nature on your private Facebook account.

It is extremely common for solicitors to utilise Facebook purely for personal reasons, and use it to share photographs of holidays and accounts of their day to day activities. It is key to understand that anything placed on Facebook, whilst it may appear private within its relaxed environment, is still subject to the Code of Conduct.

7.11 Twitter

Twitter is generally considered to be the main competitor of Facebook and most practitioners will be familiar with the site and the concept of "tweeting", purely because Twitter is more commonly employed by the legal profession than Facebook. Twitter is a social media site where users can post text based content up to a maximum of 140 characters.

Similarly to Facebook, Twitter possesses a massive network of users which law firms are equally keen to impress their services upon. Firms can set up their own Twitter accounts which can then be followed by users on Twitter in order to receive updates from the firm's page.

Generally speaking it is more common for a firm to use a Twitter account than a Facebook account, and the reasoning behind this is fairly obvious when the nature of Twitter is properly understood. By default, posts on Twitter are made public, and the public can view the profile of any individual account. This is the default setting on all Twitter accounts and will apply unless the user deactivates it by making their account "private", having a similar effect to a Facebook account in that a user's content will only be viewable to those members of the network who are authorised by that user.

Additionally, the 140 character restriction imposed by Twitter raises certain issues that solicitors will need to be aware of. Unlike other social media sites messages will have to be tailored to fit into the restricted allowance. Many users of Twitter do this simply by deleting or abbreviating words in their overall message; however as solicitors will know, altering words and phrases can alter the entire meaning of the overall sentence! This is coupled with the fact that solicitors tend to prefer long explanations of legal concept, and it is often extremely difficult to make a sophisticated legal opinion within 140 characters. To visualise this, consider shortening the last judgment you read into 140 characters.

A unique feature of Twitter is the use of the hashtag ("#"). Users are able to tag a specific word within their short posts by putting a hashtag immediately before it (for example a post about legal aid cuts may utilise the hashtag #LegalAid). Other users of Twitter will be able to search through all of the posts made to Twitter by searching hashtags, and if the same hashtag is used by a significant number of users in a short period of time then Twitter will notify other users that this specific hashtag is "trending", i.e. that a large body of Twitter users are posting about the same subject. To continue the legal aid example, during the amendments to criminal legal aid in 2012, posts primarily by the legal profession started the trend of the hashtag #SaveUKJustice.

The risks associated with a message (whether negatively or positively) "going viral" are also extrapolated with Twitter due to the fact that any message you make can be instantly posted to their own profile, known as "re-tweeting". The result of this is that any re-tweeted message is quickly seen by multiple networks outside the original poster's intended audience.

This should not put you off Twitter so long as you give thought to your ethical obligations. An unethical post can of course be disastrous when a damaging post is made on Twitter, but extremely beneficial if it is a positive and engaging sales message about the firm, hence its appeal to firms and individual solicitors!

7.12 LinkedIn

LinkedIn is a social media site that is more nuanced than Facebook, and is pitched as a bespoke social network for professionals, encouraging various professional networks to engage with one another for the purposes of doing business, offering employment and commenting upon one another's services. In the legal profession a great deal of LinkedIn is utilised for discussing legal matters and the publishing of blogs.

LinkedIn offers a similar network to Facebook in that it allows users to create a profile and post updates from that profile, with the difference being that a LinkedIn profile reads somewhat like a CV, with the user detailing their current job position and any other ongoing projects, along with their employment history, references and their skills. Other users are able to write recommendations for users on LinkedIn, and these will appear on that person's profile.

Unlike Facebook however, the entirety of a user's LinkedIn profile is viewable by any other member of LinkedIn, regardless of whether the two users are connected with one another or not. Users are also notified when a certain person views their profile, and will be given the name and job title of that person. It is, however, possible to anonymise yourself on LinkedIn, the downside of this being that you will not be notified of the people who view your profile.

LinkedIn operates a similar concept to Facebook's "friends" feature, meaning that users of LinkedIn can request to connect with other profiles on LinkedIn and become connections. Once two profiles have connected with each other they will be able to see one another's interactions on LinkedIn. For example, if one of the parties then opts to connect with another user then their connections will be notified of this. Equally, if you were to comment on a post on LinkedIn your connections would be able to see not only that you have commented on another user's post, but also view that comment.

LinkedIn is similar to Twitter in its public nature, to the extent that all posts and profiles are by default viewable by the public and any user of LinkedIn. You should be aware that this is slightly more nuanced on LinkedIn than Twitter. For example if you were to comment on a colleague's post, others who you have connected to on LinkedIn may also get a notification that you have made a comment on that person's post, even if they are not connected with the person whose post you commented on.

7.13 YouTube

YouTube is a commonly known social media platform that focuses explicitly on the creation and sharing of video content. Users create video content, typically below 10 minutes in length, and then upload it to YouTube where other users of the site are able to not only view it but also comment upon it in a public forum. YouTube is another site where the default privacy settings are such that any user of the site, regardless of whether they are a connection of the user or a member of the public, will be able to view the content uploaded. You are able to share videos on YouTube privately, but this somewhat defeats the point of the network.

YouTube is of less relevance to the legal profession than the other social media networks referred to in this chapter. This is largely for the same reason as Facebook, in that the network is more focused towards social interaction on a personal level; popular videos on YouTube tend to include music videos, reviews of video games and films and independent film makers making a name for themselves. Whilst for this reason it is less geared towards the legal profession, there is a weighty amount of legal content on YouTube, and some firms have been keen to capitalise on the large network of potential clients. YouTube is also used by some firms as a convenient way of sharing and displaying any webinars they may have produced, due to the fact that YouTube is both free and a public forum.

7.14 Online forums and social media sites which encourage discussion

We have seen that one of the key benefits of social media in the legal profession is that it affords solicitors the ability to share their experiences, whether negative or positive, in their practice areas as well as allowing them to provide their opinions on new or reformed areas of law with one another. Professional sites such as LinkedIn certainly offer a platform to do this; however there is a multitude of online forums specifically devoted and tailored to these forms of discussion.

We mentioned earlier that these online discussions can act as the "pulse of the profession", but when discussing previous experiences or offering comments on areas of reform there is a substantial risk that professional and ethical obligations could be breached as a result of these comments. Sharing your experiences and opinions invariably means drawing upon your previous experiences, and ultimately confidential information about your previous and current clients. This has the potential, albeit sometimes unintentionally, to breach client confidentiality if a post is not structured in such a way as to protect your client's confidential information. Consider the following:

Scenario: LinkedIn post

Facts

You are a family solicitor in a High Street firm. A dispute resolution solicitor who is a connection of yours on LinkedIn posts a question seeking advice on their client's prospects of an application in the family courts. You reply to the comment as the facts seem similar to a previous matter you acted on some years ago:

> *"I acted for a client with similar circumstances a few years ago. In my experience the courts are quite amenable to granting these sorts of applications in circumstances such as this. I would imagine you will be successful."*

Are there any potential issues that might arise from your comment?

Rules

Principle 2: Act with integrity.

Principle 4: Act in the best interests of each client.

Principle 5: Provide a proper standard of service to your clients.

Outcome (4.1): You keep the affairs of clients confidential unless disclosure is required or permitted by law or the client consents.

Potential ethical issues/professional breaches

You should consider that the above comment may breach the duty of confidentiality you owe to your previous client. This is because someone who knows your previous client's circumstances could identify them from your comment that you "acted for a client with similar circumstances a few years ago". This is particularly relevant on LinkedIn where your professional circles frequently mix, and there is the possibility that a connection might know your client.

Possible approaches

There are several ways to approach this situation:

- Amend your comment, removing your reference to your previous client, i.e. "In my experience the courts are quite amenable to granting these sorts of applications in circumstances such as this, so I would imagine you will be successful." This reduces the risks of another connection associating the facts with your client because it removes the association of your experience with that particular set of circumstances.

- Seek your previous client's permission to discuss the matter with the solicitor on LinkedIn, making reference to the fact you wish to expressly say you have an experience in similar circumstances.

- Privately message the solicitor with your comment rather than comment on the public post.

- Don't comment.

Suggested reaction/steps to avoid

In this instance it is probably best to amend the comment and remove the reference to you having dealt with a similar matter. This reduces the risk that someone will associate the facts with your client. You should, however, appreciate that any reference to your previous experiences may draw inferences to previous clients of yours.

The potential risk does not stop at breaching client confidentiality. A solicitor could inadvertently make a negative or offensive comment about the actions of another solicitor, and even where true, posts of this nature could quite easily breach the obligation to act with integrity or decrease the public's perception of the profession. In commenting upon these discussions a solicitor will need to consider how their and their firm's professional image might be affected by any comments made. For example, the forum and news website, www.RollOnFriday.co.uk frequently discusses the more risky "gossip" of the firms of the legal profession, but even an anonymous comment made about fellow members of the profession on sites such as these could be picked up by the media, linked back to the solicitor, and be considered as an action which brings the profession into disrepute. Whilst anonymity on online sites encourages more risky comments, it is crucial to remember that purely because a site states you are posting anonymously this is not an excuse to act unethically, or assume that your actions cannot be traced back to you.

7.15 Blogs

Blogs are (typically) short online articles written by individual solicitors which are then posted on their own websites, social media platforms or on the firm's website. Blogs can in general be about anything related to the legal profession, from commenting upon areas of law requiring reform or change in government policies, all the way to blogs listing the top ten most attractive barristers in London.

Blogs pose ethical risks in a number of ways, primarily as they will usually be more lengthy in nature than short social media posts. This is somewhat of a double-edged sword; whilst a greater length will often mean that a solicitor will consider more thoroughly the content of the work (unlike a post on social media which can be done instantaneously), the chance that some part of the content will be unethical rises exponentially.

Consider also that an individual solicitor's opinion of a certain matter might differ from their firm's; a solicitor's blog may suggest to the wider public that this is the opinion of the firm, or even the profession itself.

Blogs will be either incorporated in the firm's or solicitor's website, published on LinkedIn or hosted on an individual social media site which is dedicated to the publication of blogs.

7.16 Websites

One commonly overlooked social network (albeit somewhat of a hybrid) is of course the firm's website. A firm's website is not a social network in the traditional sense; however on most websites visitors (i.e. prospective clients) will be able to interact with the firm by reading and commenting upon the content of that site. A firm's website will usually be the first port of call for potential clients when considering which firm to instruct. Equally, when a firm is heavily featured in the media, interested parties (opponents/potential employees) will usually consider the firm's website in order to uncover further information regarding the firm. Incorrect information on a firm's website will potentially attract breaches of Outcome (8.1), that your publicity is accurate and not misleading.

7.17 Other social media platforms

This book has considered only the social media platforms which are most likely to be relevant to the legal profession; however remember that a wide variant of social media exists which utilises different mediums of networking. At the time of writing there are some 211 major social media sites worldwide! We will briefly discuss some of more frequently used social media accounts in the event that you come across them when engaging through social media;

- **Flickr**; a social network site where photographers share the works that they have produced. The default privacy setting of Flickr is that all posts are shared publicly.

- **Instagram**; social networking site where the users share personal photographs of their day to day activities. Some businesses utilise this social networking as a slightly alternative way of updating their customer base as to their day to day work or product development. The default privacy setting is that all posts on Instagram are shared publicly.

- **WordPress**; a social network dedicated to the publishing of blogs. Users are able to create a mini-website for themselves which focuses upon articles posted by that user. It tends to be more widely used by undergraduate students who are required to host their own blog sites as they do not have access to a firm's website or another posting forum.

It is important that you understand broadly the privacy settings of these social media sites if you come across them, and appreciate that the niche opportunity to market presented by these networks may encourage your firm to utilise them.

It is also worth bearing in mind that social media is an evolving market, and therefore there will no doubt be new emerging social media concepts which post-date this book, and may well be interacted through mediums that are entirely unappreciated today.

7.18 Engaging with social media ethically

It is hopefully quite clear from above that whilst social media is considered to attract ethical considerations, it carries with it a considerable amount of risk from a compliance perspective. As a result of this, engaging with social media should always be approached with certain ethical safeguards in mind.

Two Accounts: One Private and One Personal

We have seen that social media bases its foundations on interactions on a more personal level, and that the use of social media for business promotion is not the primary purpose of social media. Solicitors will manage their social media accounts in the following ways:

- An account that they utilise for personal social interactions with a network comprised of their friends and family. The privacy settings of these accounts tend to be private.

- An account that they utilise for professional interactions with a network comprised of their business contacts. The privacy settings of these accounts tend to be public.

- An account that they utilise for personal and professional interactions with a network comprised of their friends, family and business contacts. The privacy settings of these accounts are more likely to be a combination of public and private.

You will no doubt not be surprised to learn that it is the third use of social media that exposes a solicitor and their firm to the highest amount of risk. This is because it can often be difficult to appreciate where the line between personal and professional behaviour lies and where your professional obligations start and end. It can also be increasingly difficult to distinguish between casual interactions with clients and more formal communications. Many people will share photographs of their stories and experiences on their personal social media accounts, and it is probably true that every member of the profession who utilises social media for personal reasons has a post or photograph they would rather their clients did not see! In deciding whether it is appropriate to combine your private and professional accounts you should consider primarily whether this act is likely to breach your obligation under Principle 2 of the Code (to act with integrity), or Principle 6 (to maintain the trust the public places in the legal profession).

From a purely professional point of view your clients will probably consider personal updates about their solicitor's personal lives to be inappropriate; most clients will not care for updates about their solicitor's significant other, or photographs of their cat. On a more extreme note, however, images from a drunken weekend of a solicitor acting unethically, if serious enough and viewed by clients, could attract the attention of the SRA.

Of course, even when utilising a personal account with private settings you should consider that this content may either not be private (due to a settings misunderstanding) or later become public. When considering whether the content you post on your private account is appropriate it is worth asking yourself the question posed in Chapter 1:

Would you be happy for the following people to view the post you have placed on your private social media account?

- An unknown person on public transport;
- A colleague;
- A friend;
- Your supervisor;
- A journalist;
- Your partner;
- Your parents;
- A judge;
- The Solicitor's Disciplinary Tribunal.

It is therefore typically good practice for a solicitor to maintain two separate accounts:

(1) An account that they utilise for personal social interactions with a network comprised of their friends and family. The privacy settings of these accounts tend to be private.

(2) An account that they utilise for professional interactions with a network comprised of their business contacts. The privacy settings of these accounts tend to be public.

Having two accounts is effective because it allows you to consider the content you are posting and then post that to the account you consider it appropriate for, be it your professional or private account.

7.19 Understanding privacy settings

It cannot be stressed enough that **all information you share on social media may well be accessible to a much wider audience than you initially intended**, and it is therefore crucial that when you engage in any form of online interaction you fully appreciate and understand the privacy settings of the particular site you are using.

The issue of a potentially unexpected audience is amplified by the fact that social media sites rarely delete historical content you may have posted; posts you may have made to the site years ago (perhaps even before you qualified) could still be viewable to a wider audience than you intended initially! Newly qualified solicitors in particular are encouraged to review their historical posts to ensure that their accounts comply with their newly acquired ethical obligations and ensure that there is no content within it which:

- reflects badly on your own image as a solicitor;
- reflects badly on the profession itself.

It is strongly recommended that any posts that do not comply with either of the above ethical obligations are made "private", or preferably, deleted altogether.

You will have noted from the breakdowns of all the differing social media platforms that a great deal of exposure comes from not understanding the nature of social media. It is therefore vital that a firm and its individual solicitors understand and appreciate the privacy settings of each particular social media site they utilise. As we have seen this is not necessarily a straightforward lesson to learn; different sites employ different types of privacy settings, be it public posts or posts restricted to certain groups or individuals, and these settings are subject to revision and change by the site owners themselves.

In practice a firm will usually take charge of ensuring that its solicitors understand the social media sites they are using in order to promote the firm, but mitigate against any potential breaches. This means a firm will need to do two things:

(1) Understand the privacy settings of each site; and

(2) Ensure that all members of staff understand the privacy settings of each individual site they are using.

It is sensible for whoever is heading the social media management at a firm to fully familiarise themselves with the privacy settings of all social media sites typically employed by solicitors. However, even where the firm has considered and adopted the strongest privacy settings this does not necessarily mean that the information posted to the social media sites is protected. Some sites may default to public settings and even sites with the most stringent privacy settings are vulnerable to attacks by cyber criminals.

7.20 Being your client's friend

A "friend request" from a client is both a personal and professional conundrum. If you do choose to connect with a client on a social media site then you will need to evaluate whether this will affect any of your professional ethical obligations. It may well not be immediately obvious how interacting with a client on a social media site may impact upon your professional obligations. However consider the following scenario:

Scenario: LinkedIn request from client

Facts

You have recently conducted an interview with a high value and well known individual in connection with his divorce from his wife. At the interview you agreed to act for the client and he signed the necessary client care paperwork. Upon returning home from the office that evening you notice that you have a connection request from the client on LinkedIn. On your LinkedIn profile it states that you are a solicitor specialising in divorce and financial remedy.

Should you accept your client's connection request?

Rules

Principle 2: Act with integrity.

Principle 4: Act in the best interests of each client.

Outcome (4.1): You keep the affairs of clients confidential unless disclosure is required or permitted by law or the client consents.

Potential ethical issues/professional breaches

In this scenario you should consider the nature of the client in question before deciding whether or not to accept their request. If you accept the request both you and your client's connections will be able to see that you have connected, and they will be able to view your profile and your job title. Viewers, including the media, may be able to infer from this that your client are seeking advice about a divorce, which may not be public knowledge. You may well breach Principle 4 and Outcome (4.1) in accepting the connection request.

Possible approaches

You could reject your client's connection request, and this would not notify you or your client's connections that you are interacting in some way. Alternatively, you could make contact with your client before accepting or rejecting it, notifying them that you have an obligation to keep his affairs confidential, and warning him that it might be best to avoid connecting at this point in time to avoid any discovery. Your client may advise you that he does not mind this, and give his consent for the connection to go ahead, mindful of the potential issues.

Suggested reaction/steps to avoid

In this scenario it is probably preferable not to connect with the client, as you may breach Principle 4 or Outcome (4.1) by acknowledging that you have a connection with that person.

Would it make a difference if...?

Your client was to "follow you" on your professional Twitter account?

This scenario is a good example of how an ethical breach can easily occur through social media without the individual consciously intending it. The solicitor in question may not appreciate, for example, that fellow connections may be able to see their new connection, or may not appreciate that an inference could be drawn from the connection and the job title on their LinkedIn account.

But what if you were already connected with your client before they became a client? This could occur where a personal friend instructs you or your firm to act for them, or where a professional contact you have afforded a great deal of networking to finally decides to offer you the work you have been pitching for.

The situation is somewhat difficult if you have already established an online relationship with someone who later becomes a client. In these circumstances it is more acceptable to maintain that personal relationship; however you should at all times consider that the relationship you have with that person must now operate with even more awareness against the backdrop of your professional obligations.

7.21 Social media policies

Avoiding breaches of the Code of Conduct that could occur through social media can be a logistical nightmare for a firm because social media usage by employees is extremely difficult to control, particularly because social media is very commonly used by employees in non-core hours for their own personal purposes. Breaches can be committed by any employee of the firm, from a legal secretary, to paralegals, to Partners.

The Law Society has suggested that safely and ethically establishing a social media presence requires a great deal of planning and preparation through the use of policies governing the firm's parameters for social media use and the permitted engagements between employees and their professional contacts.

Robust and regularly updated policies are generally considered to be very good ways of ensuring, or demonstrating that a firm has at least attempted to ensure, that social media mistakes do not become full blown regulatory breaches. A firm should ensure that it not only has a social media policy but that it also takes active steps to review and update it on a regular basis, particularly as we now know that social media is a fluid forum and is constantly evolving. Any policy should therefore take account of the possibilities that privacy settings may change or that a completely new social media platform may enter the market.

For their own sake and the firm's, employees should also read, understand and adhere to these policies in order to ensure that they are acting within the parameters of their obligations not only to their employers, but also their professional and ethical responsibilities.

The existence of a social media policy is good practice because it not only mitigates risk, but it also provides employers with a more solid ground to take action against employees who frequently flaunt policies, and who potentially put the firm at risk through negligent and unprofessional conduct on social media. This also demonstrates to the SRA that the firm in no way endorses any unethical behaviour on social media, and has taken active steps to prevent breaches of this nature.

A firm's social media policy will not always cover purely social media and may instead expand to all "electronic communications". Consider how a social media policy may assist in the below scenario:

Scenario: Derisory emails about client

Facts

You are a solicitor in a large city firm. You are working in a team of three solicitors on a divorce for a client who you perceive to be making unreasonable demands of their ex-partner, and is generally quite short and rude to all three of you.

The two solicitors who you are working with on the case have been sending derisory emails about the client to each other, copying you in.

How should you react to this situation? Would you reply?

Rules

Principle 2: Act with integrity.

Principle 6: Behave in a way that maintains the trust the public places in you and in the provision of legal services.

Potential ethical issues/professional breaches

Offensive emails about both clients and other members of the profession can attract, and have attracted, the attention of the SDT. Offensive comments in general can attract regulatory sanctions. However, due to the easily shared nature of electronic communication, they tend to attract more issues. A few negative comments among colleagues about a client in the kitchen may never come to light, but it is easy for an email to be sent to the wrong person, shared to every firm email address or even picked up by managers during a review of staff email correspondence.

Derisory comments about your client can breach both Principle 2 (the obligation to act with integrity), but also Principle 6 because if a client (or the wider public) discovers that they are being discussed disrespectfully as a result of their giving of instructions, then this will undoubtedly reduce their trust in the provision of legal services.

You should also consider that, even if the client does not have sight of these emails, merely writing or sending them technically constitutes a breach of the Code of Conduct. In any event many would consider the negative discussion of a person in a difficult situation who is also paying for your services to be unethical. Derogatory comments towards clients over colleagues are likely to breach Principle 6 with greater severity and thus will attract a greater magnitude of potential sanctions.

Possible approaches

- Respond to your colleagues that you do not agree with their comments, and report the solicitors to your firm's compliance officer.
- Reply to your colleagues indicating that you do not wish to get involved in discussing the client in such a way and do not agree with it. You could add that they also should not respond.
- Don't reply to the email.

Suggested reaction/steps to avoid

Ideally you should report your colleague's behaviour to your firm's nominated compliance officer, indicating that you do not agree with the behaviour and are uneasy about being copied into the conversation. Certain solicitors, particularly junior ones, may be less willing to refer their colleagues and friends to the compliance officer for a multitude of reasons.

7.22 Recent developments and the future

It is interesting to note that the BSB has recently published guidelines on their website for barristers who use social media. It is not an extensive document (nor is it intended to be), but comes as a result of a number of "slip ups" on social media by barristers, including one QC whose website included a testimony that *"he could get Stevie Wonder a driver's licence"*. Whilst perhaps not quite to that extent, it is not unheard of for solicitors to exaggerate their abilities online; referring to themselves as "experts" or "the leading firm" in certain practice areas, often without any formal accreditation of this fact, and unaware that this could potentially be a misleading advertisement which would breach Outcome(8.1).

The BSB's guidelines highlight certain maxims that solicitors will see reflected in their own Code, such as the duty not to act in a way which is likely to diminish the trust and confidence which the public places in you or the profession. The BSB guidelines helpfully remind us that comments which are constructed to be offensive or demean a person are likely to diminish this trust. Indeed, the BSB recently disbarred a barrister for insinuating through Twitter that Michael Gove was *"pro-Zionist"* and *"pro-Jew"*, amongst other anti-Semitic posts. The barrister in this instance attempted to rely on the fact that he had not directly attacked anyone by addressing them on Twitter. However, this was rejected by the BSB, who focused upon the fact that the tweets, which were in the public domain, would diminish the trust and confidence the public placed in the profession. Whilst untested it is extremely probable that the SDT would take the same view as the BSB in this respect.

Interestingly, the guidelines also suggest that heated arguments and debates online are inadvisable on the basis that it may compromise the requirement for barristers to act with honesty and integrity, which is of course mimicked by Principle 2 of the Code. Certainly on LinkedIn, there can often be heated debates between solicitors regarding areas of law and if you do enter into debates of this nature on social media you should consider if any of the comments you make could fall foul of Principle 2.

The BSB guidelines also repeat warnings raised by the authors of this book that even unqualified members of the profession should consider the guidelines on the pretext that they are members of the profession and expected to adhere to the same standards as qualified members.

It is hoped that as social media becomes commonplace within the legal profession (indeed perhaps it already is) the risks associated with it will also be more easily identified by solicitors. The profession would no doubt be aided by the publication of a formal set of guidelines by the SRA. Any guidance issued formally by the SRA is likely to focus on the following areas of the Code:

(1) **Principle 6**: That comments and posts made by solicitors do not diminish the trust the public places in them. Attention would likely be focused towards thinking through each online interaction made by a solicitor at the time of publishing and reviewing historic posts.

(2) **Outcome (4.1)**: That you do not inadvertently breach the duty of confidentiality a solicitor owes to their clients through social media posts.

(3) **Outcome (8.1)**: That solicitors ensure the fast paced nature of social media does not mean that any marketing advanced through social media about themselves or their firm is misleading.

(4) **Outcome (7.2)**: Due to the complexity of social media and its various privacy settings any firm utilising social media should, in theory, have controls and systems in place to ensure compliance with the Code. Equally, any guidance is likely to suggest that firms provide social media training to their employees together with appropriate social media policies.

7.23 Conclusion

It is hoped that after reading this chapter you will appreciate that there is a great deal of ethical consideration to be afforded to social media, despite the fact that usually sites like Facebook and Twitter usually do not concern themselves with ethical considerations.

The ethical solicitor in utilising social media ethically will consider the following:

(1) They consider their ethical and regulatory obligations during **every** post they make, regardless of whether that post is made on a private or personal social media network;

(2) They understand and appreciate the particular privacy settings of each and every social media network they utilise, and keep abreast of changes in site privacy settings;

(3) Appreciate that ethical and regulatory breaches can occur in subtle and completely unintended ways, and apply caution to all online interactions;

(4) Maintain separate social media networks for personal and professional interactions on social media;

(5) Appreciate and adhere to any social media policies established by their firm.

Social network	Regularly used by the legal profession?	Default privacy setting	Specific risks
Facebook	Yes	**Private** - only connections can see posts and user profiles.	Tends to suggest a more relaxed and personal environment due to the private nature of this social network.
Twitter	Yes	**Public** - any user can see posts and user profiles.	It can be difficult to shorten complex legal points to 140 characters. Messages can go "viral" within an extremely short space of time
LinkedIn	Yes	**Public** - any user can see posts and user profiles.	Profile is public and can be viewed by anybody accessing the site.
YouTube	No	**Public** - any user can see posts and user profiles.	Rarely utilised by solicitors, and therefore the privacy settings are under-appreciated.

Social network	Regularly used by the legal profession?	Default privacy setting	Specific risks
Blogs	Yes	Will differ from site to site, but **usually public** - any user can access the post.	In drawing on previous matters to populate blogs client confidentiality can be easily breached.
Websites	Yes	**Usually public** - it would be unusual for a firm or individual to have a private website.	Incorrect information can constitute a regulatory breach due to the fact the website is always public facing.
Online forums	Yes	Will differ from site to site.	Easy to breach client confidentiality by drawing on previous experiences. Anonymity on online forums encourages more risky comments.

Chapter 8: Litigation v ADR

8.1   Is litigation ethical?

In 2015, Mr Justice Turner, dismissing a first stage application for wasted costs, bluntly summarised the unforgiving environment of litigation:

> *"A cigarette packet carries the warning that smoking can kill you. Solicitors' standard terms of business should carry a warning that litigation can cost you. For litigation is an inherently risky business: there are no certain winners; and very often even the fruits of success are never recovered…*
>
> *…The moral is caveat litigator."*[10]

It is commonly accepted amongst litigation solicitors that clients who expose themselves to the contentious environment of litigation seldom have cause to thank their lawyers at the conclusion of the process. In fact, many litigation solicitors consider it a fair result if both parties are unhappy with the end result. Whilst conveyancers will ultimately provide their clients with a new home, and commercial solicitors with a profitable business asset, the litigation process is adversarial and it offers stress, financial pressure and a result that is often short of the desired resolution. The unpredictability of litigation, coupled with the strict confines of the cost rules of the Civil Procedure Rules ("CPR"), often force a solicitor to consider difficult ethical issues.

Indeed, in undertaking to enter the arena of litigation a client will often agree, perhaps unknowingly, to suspend normal life until the conclusion of their matter. Even where the client is successful, the client may not necessarily receive an outcome or remedy they hoped for and that success was at a high cost. As a result of the Jackson reforms it is now commonplace for litigators to advise their clients that litigation is costly, lengthy and stressful. The act of conducting (or even threatening) litigation can sour even the healthiest of relationships; age old business and familial relationships alike have been irreparably shattered by litigation. The system of adversarial litigation in this country places the clients in the position of adversaries; this is very damaging in family litigation where an inquisitorial approach might be more favoured.

Litigation is expensive for the parties and for the court and the public purse; this is another reason why an inquisitorial system might be better suited to modern day litigation. As a result of this the government and the courts place heavy encouragement upon the parties utilising alternative dispute

---

[10] *Kagalovsky & Anor v Balmore Invest Ltd & Ors [2015] EWHC 1337 (QB)*

resolution ("ADR") methods to resolve disputes rather than referring their matters to the courts and tribunals. ADR is considered by many to be a less stressful and more informal medium of resolving a dispute. This is heightened in family disputes where there is a heavy emphasis towards mediation which can minimise the acrimony between the parties and for which legal aid can still be available. For this reason ADR is often, but not always, a more cost effective way of settling a dispute without irreparably damaging the relationship between the parties.

There are strong incentives to persuade parties involved in litigation to at least consider some form of ADR, either prior to the commencement of formal litigation or during it. The courts actively encourage parties to settle their matters without its involvement where possible. The CPR attaches a great deal of weight to ADR, encompassed largely by the overriding objective at Part 1.1, *"to deal with cases justly and at a proportionate cost"*. Going further than the overriding objective, CPR 1.4(2)(e) states that the court's duty to provide active case management under CPR 1.4 includes:

> *"...encouraging the parties to use an alternative dispute resolution procedure if the court considers that appropriate and facilitating the use of such procedure..."*

Because of this the commonly adopted position by solicitors regarding ADR and litigation is that litigation is bad and this could be taken to mean unethical. It is to be discouraged. Therefore ADR is good and ethical and should be facilitated and encouraged by solicitors where possible. It is arguably the case now that a trial is seen as a disappointing catastrophe due to the system in which we are forced to operate.

This chapter will consider:

(1)   The purpose of litigation and ADR from an ethical standpoint;

(2)   Whether you are ethically obliged to consider and encourage the use of ADR;

(3)   If litigation is unethical.

8.2   The purpose of litigation

Litigation offers a remedy and solution to bad behaviour in society, either criminal litigation to address criminality, civil litigation to address civil wrongdoing or family litigation to address relationship breakdown. For the most part, litigation is between citizens who are trying to protect or establish their rights. If the law has no enforcement mechanism then it ceases to have any purpose. Litigation is therefore force behind the law and possesses great weight. To put this in a more poetic context:

"Litigation is about making order out of chaos"[11]

Consider what would happen if remedies for civil breaches, such as breach of contract did not exist. If individuals were free to commit breach of contract without consequence then this would have disastrous consequences for society. If there is no sanction to face for refusing to comply with a contractual obligation, then why should anyone bother to comply?

Whilst there is a need for a system of litigation, the current adversarial system for civil and family litigation might not be best suited for fostering an ethical society.

8.3   The adversarial system

The litigation system of England and Wales is an adversarial one; each party will independently submit the best evidence available to it to support its case, then the court will weigh up the quality of this evidence and make a judgment accordingly.

Some solicitors do not agree with this approach because it can sometimes lead to injustice. Consider where one party is able to submit its best case due to deep pockets for funding solicitors and a barrister. The other party has limited means to submit a weak case. Judgment goes against the weak party; it is difficult to argue that justice has been properly done.

These arguments are countered by an individual's freedom of autonomy in litigation; that is to say that each party has the freedom to choose how to present their case, or what defence they wish to advance[12]. Some practitioners are unsettled by civil jurisdictions in which evidence is collected and adjudicated by the presiding judge because it removes the parties' autonomy of how to best plead their case.

It is important to consider these underlying issues when considering your ethical obligations to your clients as, under the adversarial system, success very much turns on the performance on the day. Systems which reject the adversarial system can be said to have the advantage that the scales of justice are not merely tipped in the favour of the party who best pleads their case. In our system, the ability to best plead a case often is incumbent upon an individual's ability to obtain legal assistance and have that assistance prepare their case. Where access to justice is difficult, an adversarial system does not offer the best ethical outcomes.

---

[11] *Fundamental Principles of Civil Procedure: Order out of Chaos in Civil Litigation in a Globalising World (Neil Andrews, Springer, 2012)*

[12] *The Downside of Procedural Reform (D Barnhizer, Solicitor's Journal, 29 March 2002, 1142)*

8.4   The ethics of the cost rules of the CPR

The enormous cost of litigation and the harsh cost rules of the CPR dominate litigation; with or without the involvement of solicitors, litigation is inherently expensive. As a result of this a litigation solicitor's initial advice to a client will often be to accept a lower sum to avoid the headache of litigation, or abandon the claim entirely. Many solicitors accept the fact that due to the recoverability of costs being set at between 60% and 75% it is uneconomical to issue proceedings for any amount below £20,000. This assumes that the other party will be in a position to pay any amount that is ordered. Once again, the system places difficult ethical burdens on the solicitor.

The progression of a litigation matter to trial is considered to be a failure in most cases. The primary reason is because of the financial cost involved. The default costs rule is that a loss at trial will mean that the losing party will be ordered to pay the successful party's costs. The cost for the government in court and judicial time is substantial. On average around 60% to 80% of all issued proceedings are likely to settle before reaching trial.

The ethical dilemmas contained within the CPR are whether the fear of costs consequences, and the incentives to deter the use of the courts, should ever pressure a person with a valid claim into settling for less than they are entitled to, or even to abandon their claim altogether. Do you have an obligation to advise your client solely on the commercial reality of bringing their claim, or should the principles of justice prevail?

Litigation solicitors have little choice but to comply with the CPR and the ethical issues that arise from these rules.

8.5   Ethical considerations of the CPR[13]

(1)   The CPR demand cooperation between the parties engaged in the dispute. This in itself is contrary to the adversarial approach of our litigation system which is being eroded;

(2)   The rules dictate that the judge actively takes part in ensuring compliance with court timetables and the setting down of directions, which conflicts with an individual's right of autonomy;

(3)   The CPR actively encourage settlement in a rigid way such that it can be said that they restrict access to justice and a court hearing[14];

---

[13] *The Downside of Procedural Reform (T Aldridge, Solicitors Journal, 29 March 2002, 1142)*

[14] *Group Litigation, Class Actions and Collective Redress: An Anniversary Reappraisal of Lord Woolf's Three Objectives, (S McGibbons) in Civil Procedure, Ten Years On (D Dwyer, Oxford University Press, 2009)*

(4)   Is it ethical to limit access to justice based on a party's financial strength?

Scenario: Part 36 offer

Facts

You act for a medium sized company, ABC Limited, who are seeking damages for breach of contract from XYZ Limited for £17,500. The claim has been issued and both parties have filed their statements of case but the court has not yet listed the matter for a Case Management Conference. Having sought counsel's advice both you and the client are aware that the prospects of success in this matter are above 75% and your client is very likely to succeed at trial.

XYZ's solicitors send you a Part 36 offer to settle for £10,000, alleging that the offer is advanced purely for commercial reasons and claim that they believe (contrary to your advice) that their client has a strong defence to your client's claim. Your costs estimate to your client is that costs to trial are likely to be £48,000. On the basis that your client wins at trial and recovers 90% of its costs, you have estimated that your client's best position (winning at trial and recovering 90% of its costs) is that its net position will be that it loses £4,800, recovering the £17,500.

From a commercial perspective, would you advise your client to accept XYZ's Part 36 offer?

From an ethical perspective, would you advise your client to accept XYZ's Part 36 offer?

Rules

The SRA principles likely to apply to this situation are:

Principle 1: Uphold the rule of law and the proper administration of justice.

Principle 4: Act in the best interests of each client.

Principle 6: Behave in a way that maintains the trust the public places in you and the provision of legal services.

Potential ethical issues/professional breaches

This is a common conflict between the commercial reality of a matter and an ethical approach. In this scenario the client is likely to win at trial, however stands to lose money in exercising their claim. There is a conflict between acting in the best interests of the client (securing the best monetary outcome) and upholding the rule of law (demonstrating that the breach by the other party can be remedied fully). On one hand it appears that the client has an ethical right to pursue and obtain a judgment in its favour and the recovery of the full amount owed to it (Principle 1). It stands to lose money pursuing this, and therefore may not be in the client's best interests (Principle 4).

Possible approaches

- Advise the client that in the circumstances it may be best to accept the Part 36 offer on the basis that the legal costs may soon outweigh the amounts being pursued. Additionally, advise the client that if the defendant is unable to pay the amount owed plus costs at trial they stand to lose the entirety of their fees.

- Advise the client that they have a good claim and should push to recover the full amount, with £10,000 being far below the amount they are fully entitled to.

Suggested reaction/steps to avoid

In this situation you best serve your client by providing them with all of the information to allow them to make an informed decision on the matter. Stressing that your client should accept the £10,000 offer purely because of costs implications might not be ethical or acting in their best interests.

Additionally, you should consider whether your client wishes to have the matter subjected to judicial scrutiny, and that upon obtaining judgment they could have other avenues of remedy available to them, such as the ability to wind up the defendant company, which may well be a desirable outcome for your client.

There is little an individual solicitor can do regarding the ethical status of the CPR, and in particular the implications of the costs rules. Solicitors simply have an obligation under those rules to advise their clients regarding ADR. However, it is important that you recognise that there is an underlying concern about the ethical standard of the costs rules because of the pressure they put on parties to settle their disputes without judicial intervention. Arguably a less favourable settlement achieved purely as a result of the fear of costs sanctions is not justice being performed.

The ethics of the costs rules is particularly relevant when we consider the fact that, however undesirable, the individual wealth of a claimant or defendant plays a large part in their prospects of success. Wealth allows individuals to present their cases on a stronger footing, and provides access to tactical offers being made. Wealthy litigants can drag cases out. Where there is no court timetable in place the ADR process is open to abuse; this is done with a view to the wealthy litigant placing pressure upon the less affluent opponent.

8.6　The ethics of ADR?

ADR is an inescapable variable in modern day litigation but is, in theory at least, an optional process. Every solicitor who acts in a litigation capacity will have to advise their client of the requirement to consider ADR as an alternative to traditional litigation. It is, however, worth considering that ADR is still in its infancy in this jurisdiction.

In some circumstances the court can award costs against a party who unreasonably refuses to consider ADR. The full reality of this is realised when you consider that this penalty can be ordered even where the party has been successful at trial[15]. We have also seen that the court has a duty under CPR 1.4(2)(e) to encourage the use of ADR, and in general solicitors are urged to do the same. This is not necessarily a negative concept; solicitors will of course be aware of the numerous advantages that certain types of ADR offer over the courts. When ADR is utilised correctly it can provide a cheaper and more expedited conclusion to litigation matters, and can usually achieve these in a private environment away from the publicity of the courts.

In family litigation, the attendance of the applicant at a Mediation Information & Assessment Meeting (MIAM) has been compulsory since 2013, when issuing certain types of application. However, solicitors who do not wish to lose their clients to the ADR processes simply do not mention the possibility that there is an alternative to court. This is dubious unethical behaviour which does nothing to help the client or the public perception of the profession. The rules are clear that there can be costs consequences if a party fails to attend the initial mediation appointment without a valid exception being claimed. The costs rules in family litigation are quite different than those in civil litigation; the family courts rarely make an order that one party pays another's costs where both litigants have acted reasonably. This means that the pressure to seriously consider ADR (or non-court dispute resolution as it is called in family litigation) is almost non-existent.

---

[15] *Dunnett v Railtrack [2002] EWCA Civ 302*

Statistics released from the Ministry of Justice show that the number of initial mediation information meetings fell by 16% in 2015 compared to 2014. In fact, after the introduction of the mandatory requirement for the applicant to attend that meeting, there was a sharp drop in these meetings taking place. Despite the introduction of legislation requiring an applicant to attend a MIAM, the numbers of applicants attending is lower than it was in 2013 when legal aid was withdrawn for most family work. If there is little access to justice then parties are not aware of the existence of ADR options and proceed straight to court. The system for parties to attend a MIAM is poorly structured, signposted and results in fewer than 10% of all issued private law children applications being preceded by attendance at the meeting. Without the threat of consequences, those with and without solicitors can do as they please. The ethical issue for family solicitors who never bring this to the attention of the client is very clear; it is not acting in the best interests of the client to deny them the right to choose a non-court route to resolve their issues.

There are rather complex ethical considerations that must be afforded to ADR options before deciding whether it is indeed suitable for your client's case. Generally speaking, because the litigation environment promotes ADR in such a positive light and provides costs sanctions, the ethical considerations can be overlooked by solicitors. There has been a reported case dealt with by the SDT where the solicitor was so sure that a matter would settle that the solicitor did not issue proceedings despite instructions to do so. In that case, the solicitor was so convinced that the client would not benefit from litigating the case that he did not tell the client that he would not or did not issue proceedings.

The matters that the solicitor should bear in mind from an ethical standpoint include:

(1) Is there a genuine commitment from the parties and the solicitors to use ADR?

(2) Is the referral to ADR an attempt to delay proceedings to enable a party to hide evidence, assets or create delay?

(3) Is the client capable of negotiating a good settlement at mediation without legal representation on the day?

(4) What type of ADR is the best for this client and this dispute?

Scenario: Lying to your client

Facts

You are a newly qualified solicitor employed in the dispute resolution department of a medium sized regional firm. You are acting for a client whose managing director is notoriously quick to litigate and he has instructed you to write a letter before action to the potential defendant on a fairly straightforward debt matter for £123,000. When you receive the reply to your letter before action by email it appears that the defendant's purported defence is extremely weak.

The potential defendant's solicitor calls you shortly after sending an email on a without prejudice basis to explain that their client is in the process of advancing what you consider to be a very sensible offer. When you explain this to your client you are instructed to ignore the prospect of settlement and issue proceedings immediately.

Your supervising solicitor has always placed great importance on settling cases where possible, always stating that the cost of litigation is rarely worth it. You also think the case will settle shortly and don't want the client to have to incur unnecessary court and solicitor's fees. You tell the client that you have issued proceedings, knowing you will receive an offer your client will accept shortly.

What has happened unethically in this situation? What should you do in this situation?

Rules

Principle 2: Act with integrity.

Principle 4: Act in the best interests of each client.

Principle 5: Provide a proper standard of service to your clients.

Principle 6: Behave in a way that maintains the trust the public places in you and in the provision of legal services.

Potential ethical issues/professional breaches

The issues within this scenario are immediately obvious. The junior solicitor has lied to the client, albeit with the intention of acting in the client's best interests (in that they believe the case will settle shortly). This is both unethical and a regulatory breach as it involves lying to the client and deceiving them as to the actual state of litigation. The fact that it is purported to be in the client's and the court's best interests is irrelevant in this scenario.

Possible approaches

Realistically there is only one option in this matter. The solicitor must self-report to the firm's compliance officer. Ultimately the firm should advise the client of the situation.

Suggested reaction/steps to avoid

This scenario may seem extreme; however there are cases where experienced solicitors have been struck off for doing this. To avoid this situation arising the fee earner should not submit to the pressures of ADR and costs, fully explaining to the client the need to consider ADR and never to deceive the client as to the status of a matter.

The ethics of this selection process is often overlooked by many solicitors who are quick to advise their clients simply to adopt their "go to" choice of ADR. For example, some lawyers favour mediation and negotiation because it generally incorporates a great deal of solicitor time which captures more work for them and therefore more fees. Other solicitors are more comfortable utilising tried and tested ADR processes rather than engaging with more novel ones. A solicitor is unlikely to suggest an ADR process that they are trained to engage in as this would lose them a client - is this ethical?

In selecting the correct route of ADR for your client you will need to have recourse to:

(1) Whether a third party is required to resolve the dispute, and if necessary:

   (a) what the role of that third party will be; and

   (b) whether the effect of the third party's decision will be binding or non-binding.

(2) The role of the solicitors during the ADR process; and

(3) The role of the law.

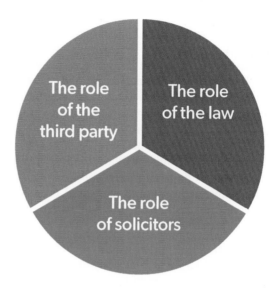

Fig 30: Considerations for selecting the appropriate method of ADR for your client

It is crucial that an ethical solicitor selecting the right form of ADR considers all three of these variables as the interaction between them will differ substantially depending upon the ADR mechanism in question. We will briefly consider the various forms of ADR which are used in England and Wales, and discuss the potential ethical issues associated with them, focusing in more detail upon the ethical considerations of negotiation, arbitration and mediation.

The primary ethical obligation to arise in the use of ADR is simply that the legal system exists for a reason. We saw in Chapter 1 that the enforcement mechanisms of the justice system operate to ensure that where people have their rights breached they are able to utilise enforcement mechanisms. It is therefore odd that the rise of ADR operates to restrict an individual's autonomy to utilise this system without being penalised. Equally, it seems contrary to our adversarial system that a person is essentially forced by the costs rules to sit down and negotiate with a party they believe has wronged them. It is even more ethically reprehensible to suggest that the wronged individual has a duty to consider accepting less than they are actually entitled to, and denying them their day in court. This ultimately means that there is a risk that the severe pressure for parties to consider and utilise ADR is in part unethical because it undermines the importance of the legal system, and a person's individual right to apply to the court for remedy where they have been wronged.

There is also an issue with the ADR mechanisms globally lacking regulation. The majority of individuals who are involved in facilitating agreements between disputing parties are unregulated, and with the exception of arbitration, ADR mechanisms generally have no regulatory framework for its users to fall back upon if their facilitators act unethically or negligently. Unethical settlements may be achieved purely because the third parties fail to understand the underlying legal issues, or are focused on achieving settlement at any cost, regardless of the legal position of the parties. In these circumstances, third parties could facilitate settlements that might work in theory for the parties, but do not actually work practically or legally. Additionally, the settlement might not take account of third parties in the same way in which a court might; for example, any children the parties may have between them or other debtors of one party.

Consider that comparatively, ADR is a private resolution process, hidden from public and judicial scrutiny. Some may think that as a result ADR has fewer ethical guidelines, and as such fewer incentives for parties to behave in an ethical way. You should be aware that, whilst an unattractive thought, there will be some solicitors who seek to utilise this hidden variable of mediation deliberately in order to obtain settlements that are more beneficial for their clients, or to avoid the scrutiny of less ethical tactics in open court. In the alternative, others may believe that because ADR is cost efficient and a low impact alternative to court, it is actually a more ethical methodology. The lack of regulation may be seen to be an adherence to a higher ethical code and this may be attractive to parties and solicitors alike.

To decide whether your ADR is suitable for your client you will need to consider all variables mentioned in this chapter, as well as whether your client has a suitable character to engage in the particular ADR process you are suggesting.

8.7   ADR processes with no third party

The most basic forms of ADR are those where no third party is involved other than the parties and their lawyers. These processes will usually involve the parties discussing potential avenues of settlement with one another directly, with or without the assistance of solicitors. Because they do not involve the expense of third parties or the hiring of venues to conduct the ADR process, they tend to be significantly cheaper than their facilitative ADR counterparts.

It is extremely tempting to assume that simply because the parties are engaging directly with one another you have no ethical considerations to make; however as we will see, this is far from the truth and can in certain circumstances be heightened purely because of the lack of a regulatory framework.

Ethical considerations

Is any potential delay to allow these negotiations going to jeopardise the preservation of evidence, assets or litigation advantage?

Is this process going to assist the parties to reach a settlement?

The solicitor should not be putting their fee target over and above the client's best interests in reaching a fair settlement early on.

8.8 Negotiation

Negotiation is arguably the most flexible and informal mechanism of ADR, depending on its approach. Many solicitors are comfortable with this type of ADR process; written and oral negotiations are fairly typical processes which can earn firms lots of fee income.

Negotiation of course does not necessarily need the involvement of solicitors. Parties involved in negotiation essentially attempt to reach an agreement between themselves. If solicitors are not instructed, then notwithstanding the personal overheads of the parties, the costs are virtually non-existent. Negotiation is normally conducted on a without prejudice basis in private, ensuring that the parties' positions are protected in the event that the discussions do not result in an agreed settlement.

Negotiation requires the consent of both parties to the dispute. It is actively encouraged by the courts and demanded in certain pre-action protocols (for example, Part 8 of the Pre-action Protocol for Construction and Engineering Disputes requires the parties to conduct a round table meeting for the purpose of narrowing the position).

The fact that negotiation offers such flexibility and a lack of official rules does of course require solicitors to be aware of certain ethical situations.

Ethical considerations

The primary purpose of a negotiation is finding your opponent's minimum position, i.e. the lowest amount that they are prepared to accept in order to bring the matter to a conclusion. This must be combined with concealing the weaknesses in your client's case. It has been suggested therefore that the test of whether a solicitor is a good negotiator is gauged on their ability to lie!

Whilst white lies permeate the daily interactions in society[16] many solicitors

---

[16] *Doing The Right Thing: An Empirical Study of Attorney Negotiation Ethics (A Hinshaw & J Alberts (2011) 16 Harvard Negotiation Law Review 95)*

are uncomfortable with the idea that a willingness to lie is central to effective negotiation[17]. The accepted ethical workaround for this is to distinguish between two different types of lies in negotiation;

- **Bad lies**. Making a statement to an opponent about evidence that you know to be untrue is clearly unethical. This will attract the attention of the SRA and if found out a solicitor will be struck off for dishonesty offences.

- **White lies**. Stating that your client is *"unwilling to settle for less than £14,000"* when they perhaps may be willing to settle for £13,000 is more likely to be considered tactical whilst technically still a lie.

Many solicitors will negotiate on the basis that *"my client has instructed me to offer £14,000"*; this makes no comment about the willingness of the client to offer more or the merits of the case. A solicitor who puts forward this offer has done nothing wrong on the fact of the facts. The solicitor may however be acting in an amoral position; being ethically neutral is in itself an ethical choice.

Some solicitors form the view that white lies are harmless in negotiation and serve to oil the gears, saving court time and reducing the costs of litigation in the process.

A common ethical consideration in negotiation is whether or not to remain silent on an issue, i.e. failing to bring an omission by your opponent to their attention. Is this ethically neutral? Generally speaking you do not owe your opponent any obligation; litigation is not a form of sport and litigators are not required to be friendly to one another.

Consider the following two mantras when considering the ethical considerations of remaining silent:

- You are under no general obligation to be open with an opposing solicitor[18].

- Silence does not constitute lying[19].

SRA Outcome (11.1) states that you should not take unfair advantage of your opponent. You will of course have to consider this against your obligation not to mislead the court at Outcome (5.1).

Finally, practitioners should beware of the "shadow of the law" that their involvement casts upon a negotiation. Generally speaking, two parties who

---

[17] *G. Wetlaufer -'The ethics of lying in negotiation' (1990) 76 Iowa Law Review 1219, 1221*

[18] *Thompson v Arnold [2007] EWHC 1875 (QB)*

[19] *Thames Trains v Adams [2006] EWHC 3291*

are negotiating directly are completely at liberty to abandon those negotiations when they please, and typically conduct their negotiation purely on what they think is fair as opposed to any underlying legal reasoning.

When solicitors become engaged in the process, however, negotiation will of course be conducted upon the basis of legal principles as opposed to the parties just agreeing "what they think is fair". Solicitors therefore drastically alter the atmosphere of the negotiation, producing a potentially different outcome. It may therefore be ethical and appropriate for you to suggest that your client negotiates without your formal assistance in the early stages of a dispute, particularly where their claim is more grounded in the fairness of the situation rather than being legally sound.

Scenario: Omission on consent order

Facts

You are a solicitor employed in the dispute resolution department of a medium sized regional firm.

You are in court for the trial of a long standing matter and are negotiating the dispute with the solicitor acting on behalf of the defendant before going into court.

After much negotiation your clients have reached a compromise and your opponent begins to draw up the consent order for the court. When your opponent hands you the consent order to approve you notice that a key definition of one of the consent order provisions has been omitted, which would make it very difficult for your client's opponent to enforce the terms of the order if your client was to default on the agreement.

Do you point out your opponent's omission, or stay silent?

Rules

Principle 2: Act with integrity

Principle 4: Act in the best interests of each client.

Principle 6: Behave in a way that maintains the trust the public places in you and in the provision of legal services.

Outcome (1.5): The service you provide to clients is competent, delivered in a timely manner and takes account of your clients' needs and circumstances.

Outcome (11.1): You do not take unfair advantage of third parties in either your professional or personal capacity.

Potential ethical/regulatory breaches

The issue in this scenario is whether it is incumbent upon you to point out errors by an opposing solicitor to the detriment of your client. You will need to balance your obligation to act in your client's best interests and provide a proper service against not taking unfair advantage of a third party. Additionally you will need to consider that this silence could be considered a controversial negotiation tactic.

Possible approaches

- Point out your opponent's error, with the reasoning being that being faced with a further complex litigation is not in the best interests of your client.
- Remain silent as you have no obligation to disclose this to your opponent and it benefits your client.

Suggested reaction/steps to avoid

This is a good example of negotiation tactics that may be regulatory compliant (silence is not lying and you have no obligation to your opponent) but is ethically controversial. The reaction therefore will depend on the solicitor, and client, in question.

Would it make a difference if you had made the omission on the consent order to the detriment of your opponent?

8.9   Mediation

Mediation is a preferred mechanism of ADR for solicitors and the courts. In a mediation process the parties meet, with the assistance of a third party ("the mediator") who will identify and narrow the issues between the parties with a view to achieving settlement.

Mediation is also conducted on a without prejudice basis and in private. Any settlements that take place within mediation are not binding upon the parties until the parties sign a settlement agreement or file the appropriate consent order with the court.

There are many different types of mediation used in England and Wales. The family model is very different to that of the commercial mediation. Thus the role of the mediator is tailored to suit the dispute in question.

The most common form of mediation in England and Wales is facilitative mediation where the mediator will actively play a role in attempting to encourage settlement between the parties by narrowing their positions. The mediator can only identify and suggest points of compromise between the parties and has no power to comment upon the merits of either party's case or make a binding agreement upon their dispute.

Ethical considerations

Mediation's popularity has risen so drastically that it has been suggested that the natural format of concluding litigation will be a hybrid between litigation and mediation, known as "liti-mediation". The parties begin their dispute with traditional litigation, but ultimately settle the matter by way of a mediation conducted after proceedings are issued[20].

Despite this widespread popularity and support, the vastly diverse body of mediators who conduct this form of ADR remains entirely unregulated. Many mediators are not required to even submit to some form of accreditation although this is starting to change. As regulation and ethics are so closely linked, it is worth noting this issue.

In theory anybody can hold themselves out to be a mediator regardless of their legal knowledge; this is regarded by some to be a benefit as the settlement of a dispute at mediation is not solely dependent on legal determination. As a result of this there is a great deal of debate amongst practitioners about whether all mediators have the requisite legal knowledge to consider more complex areas of law, and therefore consider all the potential ramifications of any settlement they are attempting to facilitate.

Ethically, mediation also falls foul of the same issues that have been made against our litigation system. A party who is unable to plead a strong case against a party who pleads a strong one may be overwhelmed with the pressure to settle. This would easily be addressed by the mediator when assessing the parties' suitability to attend mediation at the outset. In many forms of commercial mediation the parties are assisted by the lawyers throughout and any power imbalances are redressed that way.

---

[20] *J Lande - 'How will lawyering and mediation practices transform each other?' (1997) 24 Florida Law Review 839*

Scenario: Terms of a consent order

Facts

You are a family solicitor employed in a small high street firm. You act for the petitioning wife in the divorce from her husband. The parties have two young children and the husband is acting in person.

The marriage ended mutually and the couple have parted on fairly good terms, disagreeing only on a few minor points, in particular about the division of pension funds. You select a mediator who you know is very good at settling matters and has a very good understanding of pension assets. However, that mediator has very little understanding of children law which you know due to your past dealings with them.

You suggest that your client and her estranged husband attend a mediation with this mediator as you fully expect that they will reach settlement shortly and see no reason why they should engage with the court process. As expected the parties reach settlement after only one session of mediation and your client asks you to draft the consent order for submission to the court. Whilst drafting the consent order it occurs to you that your client may not be paying enough child maintenance to her husband; the parties have agreed that he will have primary residence of the children. As they have already settled on this matter you merely draft the consent order as instructed and submit it to the court.

Have you acted ethically in this situation?

Rules

Principle 2: Act with integrity.

Principle 4: Act in the best interests of each client.

Principle 6: Behave in a way that maintains the trust the public places in you and in the provision of legal services.

Outcome (1.5): The service you provide to clients is competent, delivered in a timely manner and takes account of your clients' needs and circumstances.

Outcome (11.1): You do not take unfair advantage of third parties in either your professional or personal capacity.

Indicative Behaviour (17.7): Taking unfair advantage of an opposing party's lack of legal knowledge where they have not instructed a lawyer.

Potential ethical/regulatory breaches

The issue in this scenario is twofold; whether the solicitor has acted in the client's best interests by not selecting a mediator that gives proper consideration to their client's children, and whether they have taken advantage of the unrepresented party by submitting the consent order fully aware that the opponent may be entitled to more. This is unlikely to mirror the position had the matter proceeded to trial in the courts.

Also, the solicitor has to act with integrity and by being seen to act with integrity fulfils their obligation under Principle 6. Whilst mediation may take place in private, by acting with integrity the solicitor promotes the service of mediation by showing it can be used to resolve potentially difficult issues for the mutual benefit of all parties.

Possible approaches

- Inform your client of your assessment of child maintenance, identifying that you believe she should be making higher payments.
- Attempt to retract the consent order from the court before advising your client of your revelation.

Suggested reaction/steps to avoid

Avoiding situations like this in mediation matters largely involve considering the nature of the parties and the preferred mediator. The solicitor in this matter has potentially put excessive focus on settlement and one particular part of the dispute in selecting a mediator, without reference to a mediator who would consider the needs of the children in greater detail.

A more common issue in family mediation is the solicitor selecting the mediator on the basis that they will not be able to help the parties reach a settlement, thereby protecting the client who will be forced to litigate.

Ultimately the main reason clients may wish to avoid mediation is simply because they may arrive at a settlement which is less than they are entitled to in court. There is evidence that suggests claimants receive less compensation through mediation when compared to litigation[21].

8.10 Arbitration

Arbitration is a relatively new method of ADR regulated by the Arbitration Act 1996 and it shares many similarities with the formal court-based litigation process. Arbitration has a semblance to formal litigation and it is particularly popular with commercial litigators who have been using this route for many years. It is gaining a significant amount of traction in family law as a method of resolving financial disputes on divorce and relationship breakdown. However, this is considered to be a "novel" approach in the family law arena and solicitors are hesitant to use an ADR method that they know little about. This impacts on the client's choice as the solicitor may not be wholly forthright about the availability of the process to the client.

In a similar form to mediation the process is extremely flexible, with the parties being able to conduct the hearings over Skype or by way of telephone conference, outside of core hours. If the parties agree they can both submit written submissions only and have the matter decided without the need for a hearing at all. Not only is this method more convenient but it is also normally completely private as the parties do not need to attend a public hearing centre to resolve their dispute and can attend their solicitor's office to conduct the hearings if necessary. For this reason arbitration has found much attraction between notorious members of society who would rather keep their legal disputes out of the public eye!

Arbitration is a voluntary process, but is unique in that parties can be forced to engage in the process where a clause in a contract dictates that the parties must resolve any disputes that arise under the contract by way of arbitration.

The key regulatory difference to other forms of ADR is that arbitration is regulated by the Chartered Institute of Arbitrators (CIArb).

Ethical considerations

Arbitration shares many of its core ethical dilemmas with litigation, which is unsurprising given that there are so many similarities. The major ethical concern for solicitors at the outset of an arbitration should be selecting an appropriate third party to conduct the arbitration.

This is particularly so considering that the role of the arbitrator will be tan-

---

[21] *Central London County Court Mediation Scheme (H Genn, Department for Constitutional Affairs, 1998)*

tamount to that of a judicial position; that position should be protected and an objective arbitrator should be sought. In commercial disputes this isn't such an issue as there will usually be a panel of three arbitrators, thus any bias in appointing one will be balanced out by the other two. However, in family arbitration, there is only one arbitrator and there can be a problem in the appointment process.

Scenario: Arbitration

Facts

You are a family solicitor in a medium sized practice acting for the applicant husband in a divorce. Both parties are successful business people and both want to have the matter dealt with as quickly and privately as possible. However, there are points they disagree upon such as the complex division of the business assets.

Your opponent is a family law arbitrator and has suggested that your clients engage in arbitration to settle the matter. You have no in-depth knowledge of arbitration in a family law context and understand that it is relatively novel and untested. Your client asks you for advice on this proposal. You are hesitant to suggest arbitration due to your unfamiliarity and its general novelty.

How should you advise your client?

Rules

Principle 2: Act with integrity.

Principle 4: Act in the best interests of each client.

Principle 5: Provide a proper standard of service to your clients.

Outcome (1.2): You provide services to your clients in a manner which protects their interests in their matter, subject to the proper administration of justice.

Outcome (1.4): You have the resources, skills and procedures to carry out your client's instructions.

Outcome (1.5): The service you provide to clients is competent, delivered in a timely manner and takes account of your clients' needs and circumstances.

Potential ethical issues/professional breaches

You should be cautious about rejecting *any* method of ADR simply on the basis that you do not fully understand it, or that it is a novel concept. If you fail to sufficiently consider all of your client's needs in selecting an appropriate medium of ADR then it is difficult to suggest that you are acting in the client's best interests. Equally if you do not fully understand new and evolving methods of ADR and how to apply them to your client's situation then you are unlikely to be providing a proper standard of service to your client.

Possible approaches

- Explain to your client that arbitration is a new method of ADR in family law proceedings, and as a result you are unable to recommend it to him without carrying out further research or training into arbitration.

- Advise your client that arbitration is new, and if he was to select it you may need to pass the client to someone more experienced in the practice.

Suggested reaction/steps to avoid

Where you are unable to determine the suitability of an ADR process due to your inexperience, it is crucial that you do not dismiss a method of ADR purely for this reason. The most appropriate response is to research further into arbitration to determine fully whether it is an appropriate ADR mechanism for your client. To avoid coming across this issue, if ADR is something you encounter regularly in your professional obligation, then consider ensuring that you look at all areas of ADR when undergoing your annual professional development.

Arguably, a family solicitor who knows nothing about family arbitration could not declare ongoing competency in the area of family law.

8.11 Collaborative law

Collaborative law is a type of ADR typically found within family law disputes. Each party will instruct a trained collaborative solicitor who agrees to commit their efforts to facilitating an agreement between the parties using the collaborative process. Collaborative law works through a series of without prejudice meetings held between the parties and their solicitors. At the start of the process the parties and their solicitors sign an agreement that says if the solicitors are unable to facilitate a settlement then they must cease acting for their clients. The collaborative solicitors are not permitted to litigate for clients who were committed to the collaborative process.

The method of collaborative law is that the parties organise meetings and negotiate. They are able to take legal advice during the negotiations.

The main benefit of collaborative law as a means of ADR is that it aims to preserve the relationship between the parties in a way which traditional litigation cannot due to its adversarial nature. This is of particular importance in family law matters where the parties may be required to maintain contact after settlement, for example if they have children together.

Ethical considerations

Collaborative law is a mechanism which attracts particular ethical consideration from a solicitor as it is suitable in only certain situations. Consider whether it would be inappropriate to look at collaborative law between parties who have been involved in domestic violence, where one party has not accepted that their relationship is over and therefore will find it difficult to independently focus upon settlement or there is distrust in the situation. Collaborative law, perhaps more than any other element of ADR, requires an in-depth understanding of the interaction between your client and their partner; if there is an imbalance of power between the parties there is a risk your client may well be overpowered by them. Generally, collaborative law is suited towards parties with lower levels of conflict who can focus on the best outcome for the family unit objectively with a view to obtaining a solution as opposed to a rights-based approach.

Although collaborative law was introduced as an ADR process more than a decade ago, it has not had widespread uptake by clients. Many family solicitors trained in the process but found that clients were not using it. In order to meet the perceived issues for clients, some practitioners developed a "Collaborative Lite" process. In this process the parties use the collaborative model to attempt to resolve the dispute but they don't sign the agreement at the outset. This means that if the process breaks down the parties can use the same solicitors to litigate the matter. This is deemed by purist practitioners to be unethical. The central agreement between the solicitors to the clients is that they won't litigate if the process breaks down. Those practitioners who use the process argue that they are meeting a demand and others feel that this is breaching the core tenet of the process. How can the clients trust that the solicitors are committed to a negotiated outcome if they won't sign the paperwork?

8.12 Executive tribunal

An executive tribunal is an ADR processes more commonly employed to informally resolve a dispute between two commercial bodies. A representative of each party, or their solicitor, will make representations regarding the party's case or defence to a panel comprised of the senior executives of the disputing parties. The panel will be chaired by an independent chairperson appointed by the parties, who assumes the role of the mediator. You should therefore consider the ethical considerations raised in this chapter regarding mediation in the selection of this chairperson.

After hearing the representations from the parties the panel of executives will retire to discuss the representations, with the independent chairperson exercising their role as a mediator in order to facilitate settlement between the parties. Again, here the role of the mediator is typically purely facilitative; however, again, the independent chairperson can also evaluate each party's case. In an executive tribunal the role of the mediator can sometimes go further, with the parties agreeing to the mediator becoming an arbitrator and making a binding agreement between the parties if they are unable to reach an agreement.

8.13 Conciliation

Conciliation is a variation of mediation in which a third party attempts to facilitate an agreement between the parties, with the difference being that the third party will actively pursue and encourage the parties to reach a settlement.

This is a commonly used (and mandatory) ADR process in employment disputes. You may be familiar with the conciliation process offered by ACAS in which parties must initially refer their matters to ACAS prior to issuing proceedings in the Employment Tribunal. Whilst ACAS conciliation is mandatory, in a similar way to the ethical position of the Civil Procedure Rules, you should consider whether it is appropriate for wronged employees to be forced to attempt to compromise with employers who may have caused them immense emotional pressures (the reverse situation would of course also be a consideration).

8.14 Early Neutral Evaluation

Early Neutral Evaluation ("ENE") is another variation of mediation in which the selected independent third party would provide the parties with a non-binding opinion on each party's merits after considering each party's evidence and the law in question. The parties can then decide, fully aware of their positions, to either agree to settle on the outcome of the ENE entirely, or use it as a starting point for negotiation.

In the same way as a mediation in which an assessment of each party's claim is made by the mediator, you should ensure that the party providing the ENE is sufficiently qualified to make an accurate assessment of your client's position - if an ENE is faulty and later used as a basis of settling a matter then the settlement reached is likely to be unethical.

8.15 Expert determinations

An expert determination expands upon the concept of an ENE. An expert determination is essentially an ENE provided by an expert in the field that the claim is relevant to, the distinction being that the decision of the expert is binding upon the parties. As a result of this, expert determinations are significantly more common in disputes that turn upon expert evidence to apportion liability. Expert determinations are more commonly found in disputes over contracts that involve projects like construction but can be found in low value consumer disputes such as the sale of faulty goods.

As the decision is an evaluation it is frequently interpreted as not falling within the legal framework of the Arbitration Act 1996. Therefore the only regulation involved is the general regulation imposed on experts by their respective institutes in providing their determinations.

8.16 Adjudication/Dispute Review Board

An adjudication will be used to determine the disputes which arise over the life of certain projects, most notably in larger construction projects. The adjudicator will be instructed to consider disputes as they arise during the project and make a binding decision on those disputes. This ensures that any disputed elements do not significantly jeopardise the timescale of the project.

A dispute review board is essentially a panel of adjudicators who are utilised in very large projects, typically in the construction of large commercial construction projects. The panel of three neutral adjudicators will be selected at the outset of a project and will visit the site regularly over the lifetime of the project, providing interim binding decisions on any disputes that arise during the process.

8.17 Conclusion

It seems obvious to state but the appropriate ADR method will differ from matter to matter. It would not be appropriate to state "*I always consider mediation in all of my cases*" simply to comply with your obligations to the court to consider ADR. The following table may be used as a quick reference guide to decide whether a particular method of ADR is appropriate or not:

ADR process	Third party?	Binding decision?	Ethical considerations
Negotiation	x	x	• No positive obligation for your opponent to disclose their case's weakness if not specifically noticed by you; • The atmosphere and result of abandonment will differ depending on whether your client or you conduct the negotiation.
Mediation	✓	x	• Unregulated sector; • Must ensure chosen mediator has expertise to deal with the matter; • May not adequately deal with the rights of any interested third parties.
Collaborative law	✓	x	• Ensure that your client is not leading the negotiation in the absence of your advice to obtain their best position; • Ensure there is not an imbalance of negotiating power between the parties; • Ensure there is no reason for the parties not to negotiate, such as domestic violence.
Executive tribunal	✓	x	• Are the independent experts appointed as the executive tribunal sufficiently experienced in the area of technical expertise required? • Are the independent experts appointed as the executive tribunal compliant with their own regulatory obligations?
Conciliation	✓	x	• In the case of compulsory conciliation, is it appropriate for the two parties to be actively forced to consider settlement?

ADR process	Third party?	Binding decision?	Ethical considerations
Early Neutral Evaluation	✓	✗	• Is your client's matter suitable for early neutral evaluation, or is the collection of further evidence necessary?
Arbitration	✓	✓	• Have you selected an appropriate arbitrator for your client's dispute? • Do you sufficiently appreciate the arbitration process? • Is there a risk that the matter will need to be enforced or referred to the court?
Adjudication	✓	✓	• Is the selected adjudicator suitable to deal with the dispute in question? • Is the adjudicator subject to any regulatory body?
Expert determination	✓	✓	• Is the expert sufficiently experienced in the area of the dispute to make a binding decision on the parties? • Is the expert regulated in any form?

You will note from this table that a great deal of consideration goes into ensuring that the third party is suitable for the task. It is common for solicitors to overlook this. When advising the client, is it correct to conclude that ADR is good and to be encouraged, and that litigation is bad and to be discouraged? It is unlikely that this is an ethical approach to take. At all times you should remember that litigation ultimately exists to allow wronged members of society access to an official forum which will address these wrongs if proven, and punish the individuals that have caused loss as a result of their breaches of the law. ADR can of course offer parties a more cost effective and speedier conclusion to disputes, but it is largely unregulated and private, which can be both a pro and a con.

This ultimately gives solicitors an extremely difficult question to answer: how do you behave ethically within a system which can be suggested to be unethical itself?

Chapter 9: Conclusion

Whatever the SRA's proposed dual Codes of Conduct for Solicitors in England and Wales transpire to be, it is becoming clear that the regulation of legal services will continue to emphasise outcome-focused principles with a strong requirement for solicitors to behave ethically. In modern legal practice ethics is becoming more paramount than ever.

Despite this paramountcy, this book has demonstrated that ethical concepts are often difficult to define, and differ from person to person and across generations and ethnic groups. Having read this book it is hoped that you will have gained a greater appreciation of the relationship between ethics and the law, and how this is connected to performing your regulated role as an officer of the court.

You should appreciate how your ethical obligations extend to your relationship with your clients, your regulators and the myriad of parties you will encounter throughout your legal career. You should understand that the diversity of ethical opinions, when combined with the regulatory framework of the legal profession, may mean that there may be more than one response to any given ethical conundrum. It is not necessarily the case that there will only be one right answer to any given issue.

It is also hoped that you will appreciate that ethical issues will present themselves in more subtle ways, be that in the consideration of often mandatory alternative dispute resolution media, the advertisement of a firm through social media or even the sending of emails to colleagues.

It was stated at the outset of this book that the authors intended it be used as a guidebook for practice, but it is only the starting point for developing yourself as *"the ethical solicitor"*, or *"the more ethical solicitor"*. As has been stated throughout, the intention of this book is to set out a decision-making methodology for use in practice, and instil a method of thinking in an ethical manner, with the intention of producing an ethical outcome. This should by now be very clear, and your ethical decision-making should now be at the implementation stage.

The next time an issue arises in your working day, your enhanced ethical mindset should be more alert to the potential ethical dimensions of the issue. As you think more about the ethical aspects of ordinary issues, both in and out of the work environment, the more you will realise how many decisions you will have to make in an ethical way. Self-reflection on your previous approach to ethical decision-making will allow some room for new decision making processes.

At a time where the legal profession and justice in general faces numerous threats, the need for ethics to remain strongly at the heart of what solicitors do is now more crucial than ever. If solicitors cannot be seen to act ethically then the principle of justice itself is at risk. The ethical solicitor, sitting on the Clapham omnibus, will know what the right thing to do is, act in order to achieve the right thing, and do so for the right reasons.

Know the right thing

Do the right thing

And do so for the right reason

References

The authors have consulted, and sometimes cited, the following references during the writing of this book:

Solicitors' Professional Standards: Results from the Professional Standards Survey (*Cristina Godinho (UCL) and Richard Moorhead (UCL)*)

A Behavioural Theory of Legal Ethics (*Andrew Perlman, 2015*)

Designing Ethics Indicators for Legal Services Provision (*Richard Moorhead, Victoria Hinchly, Christine Parker, David Kershaw and Soren Holm, 2012*)

Legal Risk: Definition, Management and Ethics (*Professor Richard Moorhead and Dr Steven Vaughan*)

The 2015 Ethics and Compliance Effectiveness Report

Preparatory Ethics Training for Future Solicitors (*Kim Economides and Justine Rogers, 2009*)

Independence, Representation and Risk: An Empirical Exploration of the Management of Client Relationships by Large Law Firms (*Claire Coe and Dr Steven Vaughan, 2015*)

In Professions We Trust: Fostering Virtuous Practitioners in Teaching Law and Medicine (*Phillip Bond, Elena Antonacopoulou and Adrian Pabst*)

CISI Code of Conduct

Legal Ethics at the Initial Stage: A Model Curriculum (*Professor Andrew Boon, 2010*)

Lawyers as Professionals and as Citizens: Key Roles and Responsibilities in the 21st Century (*Ben W Heineman Jr, William F Lee and David B Wilkins*)

Virtuous Character for the Practice of Law Research Report (*James Arthur, Kristjan Kristjansson, Hywel Thomas, Michael Holdsworth, Luca Badini Confalonieri and Tian Qiu*)

Index